*"If the non-profit film/video world has a wise man it is
Morrie Warshawski. He knows a great deal, carries it with
disarming ease, has the soul of a poet and the hard head of a
practical man. He sees the big picture and the small detail
with equal clarity.*

*Most how-to books are instantly disposable. Not this one. Put
it on your shelf, under your pillow, give it to your trustees,
and always have your copy handy. You'll be using it a lot."*

Brian O'Doherty
Director, Media Arts Program
NATIONAL ENDOWMENT FOR THE ARTS

SHAKING

THE MONEY TREE

HOW TO GET GRANTS AND DONATIONS
FOR FILM AND VIDEO PROJECTS

by

MORRIE WARSHAWSKI

Published by Michael Wiese Productions, 11288 Ventura Blvd., Suite 821, Studio City, CA 91604, (818) 379-8799. http://home.earthlink. net/~mwp.

Cover design by Barry Grimes, Los Angeles
Photographs by Fieldworks

Printed by Braun-Brumfield, Inc., Ann Arbor, Michigan.
Manufactured in the United States of America

ISBN 0-941188-18-3

Warshawski, Morrie.
     Shaking the money tree : how to get grants and donations for film and video projects / by Morrie Warshawski
          p.   cm.
     ISBN 0-941188-18-3
     1. Motion pictures -- United States -- Finance. 2. Video recordings - United States - Finance. I. Title.
PN1993.5.U6W33   1994
791.43'068'1--dc20
                                                      93-44541
                                                      CIP

TABLE OF CONTENTS

ACKNOWLEDGMENTS

No work of this breadth can happen in a vacuum. Because this book is the culmination of my many years of consulting, I must begin by thanking all the independent film and video producers who have shared their trials and tribulations with me and who are the true heroes of this story.

A huge debt of gratitude goes to my wife, Evy, the toughest and most supportive editor a writer could ever want.

It may be unusual to see a "thank you" note to a publisher, but I want to thank Michael Wiese here, for the record, for taking a chance on me and on this book, and his staff for its patience and advice. Also, a tip of the hat to Robin Quinn, copyeditor extraordinaire, for putting the finishing polish on this apple.

Many individuals lended support to this book either by reading rough drafts or by allowing their experiences to be included in order to help others in the field. Heartfelt thanks to all of the following: Carrie and Yasha Aginsky; Tom Ciesielka; Claudia Daugherty and Betul Ozmat of the Metropolitan Association for Philanthropy; Zeinabu irene Davis; Sally Jo Fifer at Bay Area Video Coalition; Carol Giles of the St. Louis Public Library; Sue Greenberg at St. Louis Volunteer Lawyers and Accountants for the Arts; Karen Kiss; Van McElwee; Peter Miller of Nosotros Moving Pictures; Mimi Pickering at Appalshop; Paris Poirier; Steve Ross; Kim Shelton; Gail Silva and Julie Mackaman at Film Arts Foundation; Loretta Smith; Kenji Yamamoto; and Debbie Zimmerman.

INTRODUCTION

WHY ASK WHY

Why write a book about fundraising when library and bookstore shelves sag under the weight of heavy tomes on the subject? Why try to encourage film and video producers to look for donations when money is tighter now than at any other time in recent memory?

The answer is purely selfish. As an arts consultant I usually receive a desperate call from a filmmaker just at a point of crisis. The normal plea goes something like this: "I need to raise x dollars to finish my film. I've been rejected by everybody. I can only afford two hours of your time. Please talk to me and solve all my problems - now."

After consulting with dozens of independent media makers, I've come to realize that the quick fix is usually just that - a flimsy Band-Aid often applied too late. Begin a project's life properly, and you need not apply plastic surgery later.

With that intent, I created a workshop in 1985 called HOW TO GET GRANTS AND DONATIONS FOR FILM AND VIDEO PROJECTS. I have presented this seminar in media arts centers around the country, from New York to Honolulu. The workshop prescribes a diet and regimen for media makers that helps produce vibrant, thriving fundraising plans for projects that will, with the right effort, naturally attract money.

In the workshop, and in this book, I seek to empower individuals to embark on and complete the entire process of fundraising without my help. As I often say during my workshops, my greatest wish is that I not see any of you again. If I do my job well, the information imparted here, along with its references, should guide any dedicated and determined person through the labyrinth of finding donated dollars.

SPRINTERS NEED NOT APPLY

This book aims to help long distance runners. The most effective strategies for fundraising are <u>long-term</u> strategies. Often I will advise the reader to embark on activities that will not have an immediate payback. I will be telling you to take a short-term loss and work for long-term gain.

If you are interested in quick easy money to make just one film in your life, then this is not the right book for you.

A waitress once approached me for assistance with a half-hour documentary she wanted to make on developmentally-challenged women who want to become mothers. She said, "I don't want to be a filmmaker or producer. I just need to get this one idea out of my system and go back to waitressing." In that event, my advice was for her to do the project quickly for as little as possible and then to go on with her life. To raise the money, I suggested she flash some plastic, ask her relatives to make an investment, or take out a loan.

The whole enterprise of fundraising can be a slow, debilitating process. A filmmaker must climb an incredibly steep and difficult learning and time/energy investment curve before reaching a plateau and getting that first grant check.

How much time? I warn filmmakers to gird themselves for a minimum of six months and more likely eighteen months before seeing their first grant if they start today. In addition, projects are taking longer and longer to complete primarily because money has become so hard to find. My clients can consider themselves lucky to complete a project from concept to beginning distribution in three years, with five years a more normal course of events, and seven years not unlikely.

That first pot of money will appear disproportionately small when compared to the massive mountain of effort expended on its behalf. Only over time, as you begin to look for money for your second and third projects, will that initial effort begin to make sense.

NOT FOR PROFIT

Although the strategies I will outline could be used by any artist involved in almost any kind of enterprise, I have designed this book primarily for creators of noncommercial media programs - social issue documentaries, nontraditional independent features, videoart, experimental films and short narratives.

I am going to define "noncommercial" programs as those that from their outset meet the following criteria:

1. Projects that do not <u>intend</u> to make a profit and where some other driving force is primary (e.g. social good, aesthetic achievement, education, etc.).

2. Programs where conservative initial income projections predict that distribution efforts will not return all production costs and all of the expenses of marketing and distribution.

Funders prefer projects that are inherently noncommercial in nature. That is why the issue of intent is crucial. A Hollywood producer approached me with a project and asked for my opinion of its potential to get grants. The program he intended to make would be a $5-million to $10-million feature film intended for broad distribution. In the prospectus, the producer predicted that investors would all get a handsome return on their funds. To get the project started and reduce the risk factor, this filmmaker wanted foundations to give him $500,000 in grants for research and development.

My answer was that even though foundations are happy to see filmmakers make some money in distribution, it is the rare foundation that would give money to a project that had every intention of becoming a large commercial success. A project must have a primarily noncommercial focus to get grants. I have seen noncommercial projects that ended up getting a small percentage of investment money. I was involved with a noncommercial feature, THE STAND IN (starring Danny Glover and directed by Bob Zagone), where 90% of the funds came from foundation grants and 10% from one individual as an investment. The opposite scenario, however, rarely happens. A project that is 90% backed by commercial investors will probably not find 10% from foundations.

If anywhere in the furthest recesses of the tiniest neuron hidden in the most inaccessible part of your brain there resides the thought that your project has tremendous commercial potential, save yourself the long and arduous path of grants and donations when investors are so much easier and faster to find.

YOUR SURVIVAL KIT

The filmmaker who wants to thrive in the world of grants needs a survival kit. First and foremost, create an emotional support system - an understanding significant other, a close group of friends, a sympathetic ear at your local media arts center, or even a professional counselor. You are going to experience many moments of great frustration and having a shoulder to cry on makes a tremendous difference.

For years you have been thinking of yourself as an "independent" filmmaker. But really this is a misnomer. The only truly independent filmmaker is someone who can afford to make a program without anyone's financial or technical assistance for viewing by herself in a cave without anyone else around. If this scenario does not describe you, then you are probably an "interdependent independent" filmmaker who needs to recognize the strength and value of working with others.

You are going to need an unshakable sense of purpose that creating film or video is the most effective way to fulfill your mission in life. If you have not yet created a mission statement for yourself, now is a good time to sit down and create one. For some help I can recommend Stephen R. Covey's excellent book, *The 7 Habits of Highly Effective People.* Here is my own mission statement:

"My mission as an arts consultant is to nourish the creation, proliferation and understanding of artists and their art by empowering artists, arts organizations and communities to significantly increase their administrative effectiveness."

Add to this a truly dynamic, dynamite project idea - an idea with enough depth and magnetic attraction to carry you through a few years of commitment. Slick project ideas with a slim veneer are bound to wear thin quickly. Every noncommercial project reaches a point where the filmmaker asks "Do I really want to keep working on this?" The answer will be "yes" only when the project strikes a very deep personal chord and inspires a strong sense of purpose.

For personal financial support, you are going to need a very part-time job at a very high hourly wage, an inheritance, or a significant other with a permanent full-time position. It is highly unlikely that grant income for your program will be large enough to cover all of your living expenses for the full life of the project, and substantial support rarely comes at the beginning of a project. The filmmakers I have worked with have done a number of things to survive. One actually had an inheritance; one drove a cab when finances got tight; another taught full-time at a university; one was a waitress; another worked part-time at a museum. **No one I have ever worked with makes a full-time living solely from creating their own noncommercial programs.**

To complete your survival kit, throw in a computer and appropriate software. I cannot imagine undertaking this process without access to a computer. I am not saying that you personally need to own a computer or know how to use one. However, to be effective and competitive in the grant arena you must at least have access to a computer and to someone with computer skills.

The kind of computer - Apple or IBM - makes no difference. Any computer that allows you to easily reconfigure text and play with budgets will be one-thousand times more efficient and powerful than working by hand or with a typewriter and calculator. Only a few years ago I would not have insisted on computer literacy. Now, however, it is possible for about $1,000 to buy a new computer, printer and software with more than enough power to do everything I will recommend. Also, remember your environment. You are entering an arena where everyone else is already using a computer. Access to the same powerful tools helps ensure a level playing field.

LAST WARNING

You have not purchased a grant writing book. Anyone who wants to learn the art of grant writing should turn to my bibliography and pick up any one of a number of excellent books already written on the topic. I can highly recommend, for instance, *Get the Money and Shoot: The DRI Guide to Funding Documentary Films.*

I have two theories about grant writing. The first is that learning how to write is not something that can be done quickly or easily. I used to teach writing in a former life as an English Instructor on the university level. At this point in your adult life either you know how to write lucidly or you don't. If you do know how to write, follow my instructions in Chapter 8, which contains step-by-step instructions for preparing a grant proposal.

If you don't know how to write, it could take a couple of years to get you up to speed. So you need to find someone who does have literary skills and make him or her a partner or pay a fee. The main thing is that you have a strong vision, a great project and the ability to verbally articulate that project in detail to a writer who will translate that into exciting, convincing words on a page.

My second theory is that the written grant proposal is only the tip of the iceberg. This book might more appropriately be titled *The Art of Grant Hustling* or *The Gestalt of Fundraising*. It is the rare occasion when a filmmaker receives a donation on the basis of a written proposal only. But more on that later.

This book concentrates on the strategies and activities that lead up to a written proposal - the real activities that make the difference between successful projects and ones that fizzle away. As any honest funder will tell you, two main pillars support any successful fundraising campaign - the inherent strength of the project itself and the persuasive skills of the person making the proposal. This book will help you strengthen both pillars.

DESIGNING THE PROJECT

FIRST THINGS FIRST

How does a filmmaker decide what film to make? The scenario I often hear goes like this: "I read about this incredible event (or met this amazing person) and I knew that **this was a story that had to be told.**" The story could be almost anything - the life history of someone active in the civil rights movement, the destruction of old growth forests in the Northwest, the ancient craft of making paper by hand, or a striking image from a dream that cries out for more exploration.

A deep chord is struck inside your heart and you feel compelled to make a program about that subject. At this point, do not assume that the rest of the world shares your passion. Too many filmmakers have made this mistake. The assumption is that the subject matter alone is so powerful that funders just will not be able to say "no" to a written request.

Passion for your project is wonderful. You will absolutely not be able to raise money and survive the trials of fundraising without this emotional asset. But you must wed to this passion a healthy dose of reason and research.

Many filmmakers embark on the fundraising journey with only a good idea in their pockets. It takes much more than a good idea to garner donated funds. Support this idea with lots of data and surround it with research. The biggest mistake a filmmaker can make with funders is to approach them with an idea and not be able to answer a number of basic questions about: need, audience, distribution, marketing and budgets.

Let's walk together down this path of basic questions. As you begin to answer and deal with these topics, two things will be accomplished.

The first is that you will indeed be deciding whether or not the program idea is as substantial as you first thought. This helps build up your reserve of strength for the fundraising journey. Equally as important, it may help you decide not to do the project at all.

The second is that by answering the basic questions you will essentially be writing the final grant proposal and be preparing yourself for the pitch(es) that you are going to make to funders. Being fully versed in all aspects of your project is key to creating a lucid and convincing proposal.

REINVENTING THE WHEEL

Thinking that the world needs another film or video program and proving it are two different things. Start by asking, "Has anyone else already done this program?"

I received a call from a producer who said he had a project that was sure to be popular. His program was going to be a history of radio. I asked if the producer knew that Ken Burns (*The Civil War*) had just completed a lengthy documentary on the history of radio. This producer said no, he was not aware of Ken Burns' work, and wondered if this would really be important anyway!

Well, the answer is a resounding "yes it is." Funders care a great deal about whether or not your idea, in any form, has already been turned into film or video. The reasons should be obvious. Funders are loath to fund the same idea twice. Film and video are just too expensive to create, especially when compared to everything else that funders support. Because of this, no one wants to throw a lot of money away on reinventing the wheel.

Most funders are very aware of the major films and tapes that have been created in their areas of interest. Become aware of these programs too. There are many ways to check out your competition. Consult books in the library that contain filmographies of your topic. Peruse *Bowker's Complete Video Directory* or *NICEM's Film and Video Finder*. There are information retrieval services that for a fee can do database searches by topic which you order over the phone or by mail (e.g. American Film and Video Association, Art on Film Database or PBS Videofinders - all listed in the appendix on page 116-117).

Look for titles and descriptions of other programs similar to your own idea. Find out more about these programs (read reviews, for instance) and be prepared to find a way to see the program itself. If necessary, pay to rent a VHS copy to truly educate and completely familiarize yourself with a program or two. This is especially important if the program is very well-known in the field and people will be referring to it.

If an extremely similar program has already been done, then this is a time to seriously consider jettisoning the project before getting started. What is more likely is that a lot of other work has been created in your area of interest, but nothing quite like what you envision.

DIFFERENTIATION

Funders are going to say, "Aren't there already a number of films out about 'topic z'?" In response, you are going to rattle off the titles of the key works and then enumerate the many ways that your program is going to be different.

The gambits for differentiation might include:

• **My program will be more current.** All the films on this topic are outdated and have old information.

•   **My program will be a more in-depth and extensive examination of the topic.** All the prior films were shorts, and mine will be two-hours long.

•   **My program is intended for a different audience.** All the available films on this topic are for adults, and I am designingmine for elementary school students.

•   **My program will be taking a new angle on the subject.** Everyone else has dealt with global, political solutions to the problem. I will concentrate on the things that average, ordinary individuals can do.

IS ANYBODY OUT THERE?

Every program has an audience, but no program appeals to every audience. Do not go into this project assuming that everyone, everywhere will love it. Do not go into your project with the intent of trying to please everyone.

I always ask my clients, "Who are you making this program for?" Too frequently filmmakers give the following answers: "Everybody," or, "Everybody who watches PBS." Neither answer works with funders. If you do not know who the target audience(s) will be, then how can you make intelligent decisions about program content issues? How can you talk to a distributor? How can you begin to design marketing and public relations efforts?

When Bruce Sinofsky and Joe Berlinger set out to make their documentary film *Brother's Keeper,* they were convinced they had a hot story that everyone would want to see. When they approached distributors with the finished film about a murder trial involving three elderly dairy farmers in central New York, Sinofsky and Berlinger got the cold shoulder. No distributor could figure out who would want to see the program, and none could come up with a specialized marketing plan.

"One reason no distributor would take the film is that there was no identifiable target group," Mr. Berlinger said. "So we went out to identify them."

The film makers decided that despite its quirky subject matter, Brother's Keeper could appeal to several interest groups, including bar associations, organizations devoted to rural issues and the rights of the elderly, and film clubs.

— <u>The New York Times</u>, February 16, 1993

Sinofsky and Berlinger also discovered through screenings in New York City and San Francisco, that the film had a very strong response from the elderly. Now, only after the program was made and forced into self-distribution, were the filmmakers discovering its audience.

AUDIENCE CIRCLES

You can begin the question of audience in a number of ways. The first and least effective way is to ask the following question: "Who will definitely not like or need this program?" This method is the process of elimination. I only recommend this when a filmmaker really believes that everyone everywhere will want the finished program.

To this filmmaker, I would point out a number of audiences for which the program might be totally inappropriate: the elderly indigent, children under six years of age, recent immigrants from Eastern Europe, middle-aged adults grieving the loss of a spouse, etc.

A better way to begin is with a profile of the audience you would like to reach. Try the following types of filtering categories to help define that audience:

Age,
Geographic location,
Race,
Gender,
Income,
Lifestyle,
Occupation,
Political affiliation,
Education level, and
Religious affiliation.

This process will result in a list of a number of possible audience circles. At this point, try prioritizing your list in two ways.

1. Of all the possible audiences **who do you most want to reach?** This could be either the audience which needs the information the most, or an audience that does not think it needs your program but whom you are trying to lobby or affect in some way.

2. Of all the possible audiences, **who will be the easiest and most lucrative audience to reach?** This audience is most likely to buy your program as a video cassette, to pay to see it in a theater, or to watch it on a TV venue that will pay a fair per-minute fee.

These two rankings of priorities may not be the same. Each leads to possible funding sources, funding and marketing strategies, and distribution opportunities. If, for instance, the main target audience is underserved and economically disadvantaged, then you may have to build a healthy dose of distribution subsidy into the budget to provide free copies or easy access to this audience.

The question of audience will also lead to a reconsideration of some basic production questions. If, for instance, your primary audience is young children, then should the level of language and length of scenes in the script be changed? If there is a potential international audience should you shoot in film instead of video?

THE BIG "D"

Every program enters the arena of distribution sooner or later. So why is it that filmmakers are so reluctant to talk to distributors, and often make the mistake of waiting until their programs are finished before they approach a distributor?

Talk to a distributor as early in your project as possible. An excellent place to start your research and strategy is with the *AIVF Guide to Film and Video Distributors*. Find a few distributors that handle programs similar to yours and that are familiar with the kinds of audiences you want to reach.

A distributor can be a great fount of free information for you, and also a reality check. Remember, a distributor makes a living from selling the programs you are creating. The distributor lives on the front lines of the marketplace and has a practical and realistic sense of the viability of your program.

What can distributors provide at this early stage?

• A sense of whether or not there is a need for your program in the marketplace, and what kinds of sales can be expected for each of the markets you want to reach.

• Suggestions for more effective ways of approaching the topic, or elements that might make the program different from others already available.

• A support letter to attach to grant applications. A letter from a distributor lends tremendous credibility to the viability of any program.

• If they are crazy about you and your idea, they

might even offer an advance - although this is quite rare!

•   A recommendation of another distributor who might be perfect for your program.

FEAR OF FAILURE

A young client approached me once with a program that had very limited audience potential. I asked if he had talked to any distributors yet and he said he had not. I am quite used to filmmakers not talking to distributors, but usually because it is an oversight. In this instance, the filmmaker said he had made a conscious decision not to call any distributors because he was afraid of what they might say.

I am going to assume that everyone reading this book is an adult. We may not all be mature adults, but we have to be capable of taking in all kinds of information. We then either reject it and move on, or accept it and make the necessary changes to be more effective at what we do.

If there is no interest in reaching anyone with your program, then there is no need to contact a distributor. If you want to have a program that lives a full life in the world and actually gets seen by your prime audience, start your journey with the destination in mind.

Another of my clients was working on a very large project, three one-hour documentaries about the environment. When I asked about his primary audience, he said it was high school and college students. I sent him to a distributor familiar with that market just to test out the idea.

The distributor had some important points to

make. The first was that this particular slant on the environment was perfect for this age group. To the knowledge of this distributor, no other program like it existed, and he was sure it would do well in schools. This news made the filmmaker very happy.

The second important thing the distributor said was that he could not use three one-hour films! The length was inappropriate for the intended audience. He counseled the filmmaker to consider natural breaks at either 20-minute or 30-minute intervals so that the work would fit into normal classroom schedules.

I was on a panel recently with Debbie Zimmerman of Women Make Movies. She reminded the audience of two concepts that filmmakers sometimes ignore. Debbie informed filmmakers that there are three things you can try to obtain from distribution - "Fame, fortune or a good conscience." It is rare, she said, that you can attain all three.

Her other point was that filmmakers need to realize the difference between "audience" and "market." A distributor can only spend time and money dealing with markets (e.g. schools, institutions, cable, etc.). If your audience has no easily accessible market, then you will need grants and subsidies to reach them.

TIME AND MONEY

LIFESTYLE

How will you conduct your life while creating your project? Approximately how much time should you allocate to each phase of your work? Begin to consider the following elements of the film and the style of work you will engage in for maximum results:

• **Research**: Is this a project that will entail a great deal of research? In libraries or in the field? Will you have to involve specialists in your research? Will they come to you or will you have to travel to see them? Are you going to have to create a script before shooting or will a treatment suffice?

• **Production**: Is this a shoot that can happen easily in a local setting, or do you need to go to a community where you must live for a long period of time in order to gain the confidence of your subjects? Will shooting happen in one chunk, or do you have to shoot in spurts over a number of months?

• **Post Production**: Do you have easy access to appropriate equipment and skilled editors in your city? Will you need to sequester yourself for a long period of time to do the edit, and where will it happen? Are you going to involve experts or focus groups in your editing process before the final cut?

• **Fundraising**: Who is going to raise the money for the project? How much time, energy and money will you expend looking for funds? Can you raise most of the money locally or will you have to travel to find support? (I will help you find answers to these questions later in the book.)

• **Distribution/Marketing**: Is it your intent to work full time at distributing the project once it is completed?

Will you commit resources to entering and attending festivals or conferences to promote your work? If you give your program to a distributor, how much time will you devote to helping that distributor promote your work?

Nothing in life is totally predictable. Whatever scenario you imagine at the beginning of your project will change throughout the project's life. But begin the project by showing funders you have a realistic sense of the potential total commitment your film or video will demand.

GOOD COMPANY

Few rules or equations apply to fundraising for independent films and videos. Almost everything falls into a grey area. When it comes to you and your crew, however, one equation does hold true in attracting grants:

<u>The less established and experienced you are, the more well-known and experienced your crew must be. The more well-known and experienced you are, the less established and experienced your crew needs to be.</u>

Some funders do make it their business to seek out and assist emerging media artists who show talent and potential but are new to the field. These funders are rarities. Most funders, and most individuals who give money to projects, want to know that the project has a high probability for success. The more experienced and successful you and your crew have been in the past, the more credible you become in the eyes of funders. Your task as a media artist looking for funds is to suffuse all efforts and materials with an aura of credibility.

One way for young, emerging or first-time directors or producers to do this is to surround themselves with a crew that has impeccable credentials. This might mean hiring a cinematographer who has worked on award-winning projects, or an editor with a history of excellence in the field.

At one of my seminars a young filmmaker asked, "What if I am doing experimental work and I want to work only with other young and inexperienced artists?" In that case, find a well-respected artist with a national or international reputation who would sign on to be an advisor or consultant to the project. As the filmmaker, you still retain total artistic control. At the same time, the funder has a comfort zone knowing that a seasoned professional will be around for help when and if you need it.

Early in the deliberations decide what specific roles you will play in the project. Are you Executive Producer, Producer, Director, Writer, Cinematographer, Editor, and/or Distributor? Begin to find people to fill whatever roles you do no wish to take on yourself. Select the right people for the project you have in mind.

I have seen producers approach funders with projects that do not yet have crews. This will work only if you are still in the planning stage and are looking for research, development or script development funds. Once you begin to ask for production funds it is essential to name the people who will have key roles in your project. Crew member and your significant participants should provide you with signed letters giving you permission to include them in proposals.

GOOD TIMING

Funders will want to know how long the entire project will take to complete, and how much time each of its phases will eat up. At the beginning of the process, plan time liberally. Assume that everything will take longer than you think. One of the great problems that funders have with media projects is that productions are rarely completed on time. You are much better off finishing earlier than the predicted end date than later.

The time line you create should provide an accurate projection of how long the project would take from conception through distribution if there were no interruptions. Of course, there will be interruptions. That is why I recommend a time line that is not tied to specific dates but rather lists generic weeks, months and years for each activity. Let's say you promise that post-production will begin on January 15th, for instance, but then you get a paying job offer that postpones activity for two months. A specific time line would then be out-of-date and would have to be reprinted.

Here is an example of how a simple time line might look.

TIME LINE

Year 1   *Year 2*
Months 1 2 3 4 5 6 7 8 9 10 11 12 1 2 3 4 5 6 7 8 9 10 11 12

ACTIVITY
Fundraising x——————————————-x
Research   x—-x
Scripting   x—x
Production   x——-x
Post Production
  Off-Line   x————————-x
  On-Line   x
Distribution
  Festivals   x————————-x
  Theatrical   x————————-x

Your time line will be more detailed than this, and it will probably include more time. The useful thing about this type of generic graph is that wherever you are in the project you can see how much time it will take to finish if there were no interruptions. For instance, if you get stalled for six months after production ends because money has run out, you can tell funders that with full finishing funds you can complete the project in seven more months. The time line also helps you evaluate your lifestyle and time commitment needed before completion. It is just one more reality check before you jump into the rocky waters of fundraising and start swimming upstream.

MORRIE'S (COMPUTER) BUDGET TIRADE

Now you can begin the process of putting together the initial financial forecasts for your project. First and foremost: **use a computer!**

When you try to create your budget by hand on a columnar pad with the aid of a calculator it is as if you are still driving a horse and buggy cross country while everybody else is on a jet plane zipping from coast to coast. Even the cheapest budgeting or spreadsheet program on a low-powered, used computer will give you much more flexibility and power than any calculator ever could. For a detailed description of how to configure budgets and use a computer try Michael Wiese's excellent book *Film & Video Budgets*.

A particularly important benefit of figuring a budget on a computer is the ability to change any one item and instantly see the consequences on the entire budget. This type of flexibility - the capability to easily and endlessly play "what if" - is absolutely essential to your ability to jump in different directions and do accurate planning throughout the life of the project.

The computer will also save many hours of time (and therefore money) during fundraising as you reconfigure different sections of the budget for different funders and as you begin to update the budget each time you get a grant, earn income or firm up expenses.

There are many software programs available that deal with film/video scripting and budgeting. If you have a lot of money, any of them will work fine. There are also many financial forecasting, budgeting, accounting and spreadsheet programs that are very easy to use and will work as well (Lotus 123, EXCEL, etc.).

I bought my youngest daughter an Apple IIe with a printer and software for $200 at a garage sale recently. It has more than enough power to churn out the kinds of budgets you will need. So money is no excuse not to enter this arena. Even minimum proficiency with any of these software packages will allow you to knock out a template for current and future budgets in a few hours.

YOUR FIRST BUDGET(S)

I will discuss budgets once again in Chapter 8 which looks at a full proposal. At this point in your project, before you begin fundraising, try creating two budgets. The first budget will be a complete, detailed, as-accurate-as-possible estimate of what every item would cost if you were to create the ideal version of your program and had to pay for everything. This budget will form the basis of fundraising efforts and will be the budget you eventually make public.

The second budget is a worst case scenario version. Go back into the first budget line by line, item by item, and ask the following question: **"Where and how could I cut costs, defer payments, get in-kind donations and still create the program I want with integrity?"** At this point, the power of the computer will make itself evident.

File away this second budget and look at it occasionally. It is your bottom line. After you have raised 75% of your ideal budget and have hit a stone wall, this second budget will be there ready to help you decide whether to keep looking for money or to stop and finish the project with the resources in-hand. In the real world, you will probably end up working with a budget somewhere comfortably between the two budgets you created.

The notion of maintaining integrity must remain central to this process. You are creating a program that is not driven by a profit motive. Do not let budget constraints force you into compromising vision and integrity. Availability of funds will be only one factor, and not the overriding factor, in the creative decisions you make about the project.

Fundraising difficulties, for instance, may make you want to consider creating a 47-minute piece instead of a 58-minute piece. But a more crucial factor in your decision should be whether or not this shorter time length could still be appropriate and effective for the audience and markets you want to reach. With your worst case scenario budget in hand, draw a line in the ground and stand firmly behind it.

SOME BUDGET NOTES

Here are some principles and definitions to keep in mind as you create your budgets.

PAY YOURSELF! Funders hate to see budgets where filmmakers have either completely left themselves out of the budget, or where they have grossly undervalued their time. This makes you very suspect in the eyes of funders. They might wonder, for instance, if you are independently wealthy. They could wonder if you are very inexperienced and think your time is really not worth anything.

If you do not begin your budget process with the hope and assumption that you will get paid, then you will not get paid for your time. When you begin the process of having to shave costs from your project, like most filmmakers, you will probably end up trimming your salary first. But you must begin the budget process by assuming some rate of pay for your time.

Keep in mind that once you have given time to a project for free it is very difficult to go to a funder and ask for a grant to cover that salary. Funders do not like to "backward fund." Generally they do not want to deal with debts and deficits. They prefer to "forward fund" - to pay for the next chunk of your project.

I worked with a filmmaker who had spent six years on a project and never paid himself. He had raised enough money to go ahead and do post-production, but he did not want to proceed until he got grants to cover the time he had already put into the project. At this point, the answer was that he would have to consider his time spent to date as a deferral that would have to come out of potential distribution income. It just will not work to approach a funder and say "Please pay me for the last six years of my life."

COMPARABLE AND FAIR: Do not low-ball or high-ball items in your budget. My guidance here about evaluating costs is to set a price for every item in your budget which is fair, reasonable and comparable for your part of the country. In determining wages for personnel, consider their skill level and experience.

Funders often have difficulty reading film and video budgets, and it is not unusual for them to send your budget to an expert in the field. You will not serve your cause by being wildly off-base on any item. If you pad your budget with unnecessary items and exorbitant rates, for instance, funders will feel they are being cheated.

On the other hand, if you low-ball your budget, funders will doubt your professionalism and your ability to complete the project. The budget is one concrete area of your proposal that gives you a chance to demonstrate in black-and-white that you are a credible professional. More importantly, if you low-ball, you will only end up doing yourself harm by having to cut too many corners or by having to extend your fundraising beyond the schedule of your original time line.

A funder in Northern California once called me with a problem. The funder was reviewing a video documentary proposal that he liked, but this foundation had never funded a media project before. While the Board of Trustees liked the narrative, they thought the budget was a bit extreme. I asked what they meant, and they said, "Well the filmmaker is doing a one-hour video and she wants $80,000 to do the project."

I told the foundation that I could not pass judgment without seeing the proposal and budget detail, but that this amount of money was not at all unusual for this type of project. In fact, once I did look at the budget I informed the foundation that they would be getting a bargain and might consider throwing in some extra funds!

IN-KIND DONATIONS. The term "in-kind" means those goods and services that are given to the project without remuneration. If someone provides time to the project for free or if a business donates a piece of equipment, these are in-kind donations. Your budget should identify an in-kind section of expenses and then detail the source of these items as in-kind in the income section. On the whole, it is not smart to show in-kind as a major portion of your budget. There are some exceptions.

In-kind can be an excellent way to show funders initial community support for your project in the early phases of fundraising before you get actual cash donations. It lets funders know that others in the community value your work. Also, for low-budget, grassroots projects, in-kind can be a crucial and substantial form of support. Most funders can appreciate this.

31

DISTRIBUTION. Please do not forget to include at least some start-up costs for marketing and distribution in your budget. This is one of the most frequent errors in the fundraising budgets I see. At the very least, you want to show funders that you will begin the process of paying for and dealing with packaging, festivals, marketing materials, press packets, etc. In fact, even if you intend to find a distributor, you probably will have to make these expenses. It's better to plan for them now than be caught short later.

CONTINGENCY. In the for-profit, commercial, media production world, it is normal to build in a percentage contingency at the end of your budget. In the not-for-profit world, this is highly unusual. You absolutely do need to think about contingency. **My advice is to build a fair percentage into every item throughout your proposal, but not to show contingency as a separate line item.**

Funders live in a world dominated by social service agencies and arts groups that configure project budgets that never show a line for a contingency. So, a funder unfamiliar with the film and video world sees the amount for contingency in your budget and thinks, "Why can't they accurately predict what their costs will be? If they show a contingency, they must not know what they are doing."

The other thing funders sometimes do is just take a red pencil and subtract the amount of contingency from your total budget. Their theory is, "Why should I fund an item that may not even be needed to do the project? If I give the filmmakers contingency funds of course they will spend them. If I don't, then they might do just as well without the money."

The only exceptions to this rule are when a funder specifically asks you to give a contingency, and/or when you are dealing with a funder who is very familiar with film and video projects. If you are working with a commercially available film/video budget spreadsheet, then you may have to alter its format to deal with this issue.

INCOME. At this point in the project, you may not be ready to begin predicting where your income will come from unless you have done a number of earlier projects. The rest of this book is going to help you deal with this issue.

However, it is never too early to realize that every budget has both an Expense and Income side. Soon you will have to make some plans about how much **earned income** you will generate for your project (e.g. sales of T-shirts, posters, pre-sales to various markets, etc.) and how much **unearned income** you will need to go out and fundraise (e.g. grants, special events, individual donations, etc.).

WHO'S GOT THE MONEY?

CUTTING UP THE PIE

Moving ahead now with clear vision of your total project and a firm commitment to creating that vision, you have already laid the groundwork for everything else that follows. There remains just one more important activity to tackle before you begin your research and start to approach funders - levitation.

Rarely in the funding world does a donor give enough money to cover the entire costs of a program. Donors, in fact, seldom give money for "general operating support" to be used in any way you wish. Funders more commonly provide money to support specific aspects of your work.

Non-profit arts and social service institutions usually come to a foundation and request dollars for creating a specific "project" - a weekend workshop, the purchase of ten new wheelchairs, or performances in the schools for three months. These organizations are usually precluded from coming to a funder and saying, "My total annual operating budget is $700,000. Please give us support."

Funders shy away from this type of general operating request because: 1. it does not target their dollars in a way that makes the gift seem significant, 2. it is hard to see specific outcomes, 3. it does not show support from other funding partners, and 4. it leaves open the possibility that the organization may want on-going, basic operating support ad infinitum.

EIGHT MILES HIGH

The significance for filmmakers is that we too must use a "project" approach when looking for funds.

35

One way to do this is to levitate above your program. Pretend you are a neutral entity floating eight miles above the program. Look down and see the program as a complicated landscape - an aerial map made up of various nations and states.

Each of these territories can become a project ready for funding opportunities. An easy way to discover these projects is to go through your budget looking for the chronological phases of the program or for specific line items. Here is a catalog of the types of "projects" that you can fund:

- Research and development,

- Script development and writing,

- Special consultants,

- Production including travel, equipment rental, crew salaries, tape and film stock, talent, a particular shoot or interview, etc., and

- Post Production including off-line and on-line edit suite rentals, film processing, sound, music rights, archival material purchase, etc.

Anything listed in your budget can become fair game for a funding gambit. Are there any items that funders tend to dislike? Yes, there are a couple. Capital expenditures, for instance, make most funders nervous. Rarely will a funder give money for buying a piece of equipment, even if an outright purchase would be cheaper than leasing or renting in the long term. Fundraising expenses and deficits are other unpopular items in the funding community.

Another area that holds a wealth of funding possibilities lies is distribution. Funders who are nervous about funding productions because they fear failure, are more open than ever to funding distribution. Projects in this phase of your program might include:

- The creation of special marketing materials and package design,

- The duplication of copies to be distributed for free to the funders' constituents or other special constituencies (libraries, associations, schools, individuals, etc.),

- Tri-standard transfer for foreign distribution,

- Study guides for school markets,

- Lecture/demonstration programs that bring you, along with your work, to rural and under-served communities,

- Closed-captioning for the hearing impaired,

- Sponsorship for public television or cable television airing, and

- The purchase of targeted mailing lists.

With these projects in mind, you are now prepared to provide any potential funder (who likes you and your project) with a number of options for providing support.

FUNDING SOURCES

It is fairly easy to locate the general sources of funding for noncommercial projects. The difficult job is to sort through these, find just the right ones, and approach them effectively. Briefly, a filmmaker looking for money will end up requesting support from one or more of the following worlds:

- The Government,
- Private foundations,
- Corporations,
- Individuals, and/or
- Miscellaneous sources, such as non-profit organizations, small businesses and special events.

Traditionally, filmmakers have relied primarily on government and private foundations for support. As of this writing, funding for the arts from the government, private foundations and corporations has begun to decrease. Fewer dollars fill the coffers of these sources while increasing numbers of grants seekers compete for the pot.

This means that filmmakers need to be smarter and more professional than ever about their funding strategies and proposals. It also means that filmmakers must consider diversifying their sources of support to help ensure success. You may hamper your project by expecting all of your support to come from foundations, for instance. Smarter strategies include a variety of funding sources.

Let's take a quick, broad look at some of these sources before we talk about nuts-and-bolts research tools and methods. I want to let you see the breadth of the landscape for funding and provide a few sketches. You and your project are not yet ready to approach any of these sources. A great deal of research is still needed before configuring your proposal appropriately.

UNCLE SAM

Government funding can take place on a national, state or local level. Some national sources include: the National Endowment for the Arts (NEA), the National Endowment for the Humanities (NEH), the Corporation for Public Broadcasting (CPB), the National Science Foundation and (occasionally) various other agencies such as the Forest Service.

State sources might encompass: State Arts Agencies, State Humanities Councils and miscellaneous agencies such as those that deal with economic development.

Very occasionally city government entities will give out media funds on a local level through a City Arts Council, a Hotel Tax Fund, or a Public Benefit Fund that uses cable revenues.

Do not assume that all of these sources require the same type of approach or materials just because they dole out government funds. The NEA Media Arts Program, for instance, requires a very simple application based primarily on a film or tape sample, while the NEH Media Program will ask you to create a lengthy and detailed master's thesis. NEH has one of the most demanding applications of any funder in the US!

The upside to the NEH is that they can provide full funding for large projects. The NEH is also one of the few funders that is interested in funding planning, research and script development.

At the NEA, it is not only the Media Arts Program and its Regional Fellowship satellites that have an interest in media. One of my clients recently received a $35,000 research and development grant from the Folk Arts Program of the NEA for a documentary on accordion player *Frank Yankovic, America's Polka King*. You might also check out the Design Arts Program, which has funded film in the past.

On the state level, the various state arts councils are not well known for supporting media (with the exception of a few states like New York). The state humanities councils, however, have a long history of support for media projects that demonstrate a strong humanities bent and involve scholars. Filmmakers working on a project of national or multi-state scope can often get grants from a couple of humanities councils. These grants are usually in the $5,000 to $15,000 range.

FOUNDATIONS

The US contains an immense variety of foundations. They run the gamut from small family foundations to community foundations, from ones with large professional staffs to ones with no staffs at all, and from those with national interests to others whose scopes are on a city or county level.

The foundation world is where many filmmakers find most of their money. For experimental film and video artists, there are only a handful of foundation and government funding sources where support can be found regularly.

Much of this book will be devoted to showing you how to find the right foundation, how to talk to that foundation, and then how to make an appropriate application. As a grantseeker, you will find that the wonderful thing about foundations is that there is a wealth of accessible written information available about them - their area of focus, contact person, application procedures, past giving history, etc.

CORPORATIONS

There is much less data available about the corporate funding world than the foundation or government funding arenas.

On the other hand, corporate funding is a very interesting environment to explore because it presents so many possible doors of entry. A corporation, for instance, might be approachable from any or all of the following doors:

- A corporate foundation,

- An advertising/marketing department,

- A public relations/community relations department,

- The corporate communications department, and/or

- The employee benefits and relations department.

Whichever door or doors you choose, the overriding motive in the corporate world is self-interest and publicity. While you are doing research and program planning, begin to think about whether or not your work could provide positive community relations opportunities for a corporate entity.

Also, early in this process, make a basic decision about whether or not you are going to take a stand on corporate ethics and exactly what criteria will apply for deciding which types of corporations you feel comfortable approaching. Always seek to stay in a funding environment where you can maintain integrity.

INDIVIDUALS

Professionals who do fundraising for a living often cite the fact that 86% of all contributions for non-profit endeavors come from individuals. Be aware that this statistic is skewed a bit because much of this money is going to religious organizations.

Still it is interesting to note that in my experience with filmmakers the vast majority of their support flows from grant-making organizations and not from individuals. I am telling all my clients that a major area of growth for donations to media projects - until the government or the economy goes through significant changes - lies with individuals.

I will talk at length about fundraising from individuals in Chapter 10. At this point, you should begin thinking about people you currently know, or could get to know, who have money or can provide access to others who have money. If and when you approach individuals for funds, it will probably be through a one-on-one contact, fundraising parties or direct mail.

MISCELLANEOUS SOURCES

Non-profit organizations have entered the field as viable new sources of funds for programs. These include some media arts centers that do regranting of federal monies or have set up their own endowments for supporting filmmakers (Film Arts Foundation, American Film Institute, Southwest Alternate Media Project and others). A new and large player in the field is a CPB funded entity, the Independent Television Service (ITVS).

Small businesses can be lured into providing support for programs. This usually happens for modestly budgeted programs where there is strong local content that will affect a specific community. I also see small business support when there is a close connection between the filmmaker and the family that owns a small business!

Another avenue is the special fundraising benefit: a screening of a first-run feature, a work-in-progress screening of the proposed film, a picnic, a garage sale, or an auction. I am not a fan of this kind of fundraising. Quite often filmmakers only break even or make just a little bit of money from an event that can be very labor intensive. You also run the risk of losing money on these events. However, do not discount this kind of fundraising if it is appropriate, has a high likelihood of success (e.g. returns at least a 40% profit), and has the backing of a donor for basic expenses through cash or in-kind donations.

Now we are ready to begin some basic research on potential funders.

WHERE TO FIND THE INFORMATION

SHALL WE DANCE?

We have sketched some initial portraits of your program and drawn in the landscape of funding. Before writing the grant and asking for the money, you are going to need to look at possible funding sources very closely in order to find the right ones for your project.

Novice grantseekers often make one of the cardinal mistakes of fundraising; they employ a "shotgun" approach. Under this method a filmmaker writes one proposal, makes many copies and then shotguns the proposal out to a large number of funders. You could not find a faster route to failure.

The dance that is about to take place with a funder resembles the dance someone might undertake with a potential mate. If the band is playing the cha-cha-cha when you step onto the dance floor, one partner had better not be swiveling hips to the merengue or the twist. Look the dance partner in the eye, speak the partner's language, and make that person believe you are the only two people on the floor.

Efforts to fund the independent feature *Stand and Deliver* provide an excellent example of the shotgun approach. First time filmmakers Tom Musca and Ramon Menendez discovered the story of high school calculus teacher Jaime Escalante. After receiving some script development funds from *American Playhouse*, Musca and Menendez decided to look for production money from foundations. They created a bound, 40-page proposal, sent it to 240, funders and sat back waiting for the phone to ring or the checks to roll in.

Almost all of these funders did not even bother to reply. Just one - the National Science Foundation - ended up giving the film a modest grant. The filmmakers had not completed their homework assignment. They gathered together a hefty list of potential funders. But that is merely the first step in funding research. **Your next step must be to learn as much as possible about each of these funders and then tailor each request differently and specifically to every foundation.**

When most funders received the *Stand and Deliver* proposal they had no reason to take it seriously. The generic packaging made it clear that the filmmakers had not paid attention to the particular needs, interests and guidelines of the funder. The filmmakers had sent T-bone steaks to a group of strict vegetarians. For a full description of how *Stand and Deliver* finally attracted financing, order a Benton Foundation case study bulletin: *Independent Features* (see bibliography on page 112).

WHERE ARE THEY HIDING?

Wherever a filmmaker may live in the US there is the potential for numerous avenues of finding information about who has money and what they like to fund. Do not pursue funds from the government, foundations and corporations without doing some very basic homework. This work can take place in spurts of intense detective work at a library. But much of the research should be an on-going part of your lifestyle as a filmmaker. Let's look at where and how a filmmaker can become a funding-literate grant hustler. For addresses and phone numbers, just turn to the extensive bibliography at the end of this book.

•**FOUNDATION CENTER LIBRARIES:** The Foundation Center operates fully-equipped, funding resource libraries in New York City, Cleveland, Washington, DC and San Francisco. The Foundation Center also maintains an extensive Cooperating Collections Network throughout the US. These libraries are excellent places to spend the day doing basic research. The libraries contain basic texts on how to do grant writing, key reference books, foundation annual reports, and periodicals. They also provide trained staff who can set you off in the right direction. You will probably spend a lot of time with the following texts: *The Foundation Directory, The Foundation Grants Index*, and *Source Book Profiles*. For other reference materials, see the bibliography starting on page 109.

• **PUBLIC LIBRARIES:** Often a local public library will house basic foundation and fundraising books even if they are not a participating Cooperating Collection of the Foundation Center. A local librarian may lead you in production directions that might not be apparent at first. Many libraries subscribe to an on-line service called DIALOG that contains the Foundation Center's databases. You may also want to look through reference books that list associations, Who's Who biographies of trustees and CEOs, catalogs of specialized periodicals, data on national or local corporations, and back issues of newspapers and magazines. Any of these might become funding leads.

• **MEDIA ARTS CENTERS:** The great unsung heroes of the noncommercial media world are littered across the country in the guise of friendly media arts centers. Organizations like the Association of Independent Video and Filmmakers (AIVF) in New York City, Bay Area Video Coalition and Film Arts Foundation in San Francisco, and 911 in Seattle have devoted themselves for many years to helping independent film and video makers. Become a member, and visit these centers frequently. Once there you will find bulletin boards, publications, sample grants, workshops on grant writing, other filmmakers and a staff that might lend professional advice or some gentle words of encouragement. Keep the media center's staff informed about your project in case they hear of any funding opportunities. Media arts centers that provide services to film and videomakers are listed in the appendix beginning on page 118.

• **Non-profit ORGANIZATIONS:** Every non-profit organization has to look for grants and donations just like you do. Many of these organizations have their own extensive development departments and often their own fundraising libraries. Non-profit organizations in your area might include: museums, hospitals, art galleries, public radio and television stations, and social service agencies. If you have a friend or a connection at any of these places, you might be able to get access to their information resources. When I ran the Bay Area Video Coalition (BAVC) in San Francisco, I frequently visited KQED and thumbed through their copy of the *Taft Corporate Directory*. At the end of every year when KQED replaced their books, they gave me their old texts to add to the funding library at BAVC.

• **PRINT:** Part of everyday life as a filmmaking professional must be to stay current with the key publications of the trade. Begin the process of regularly perusing magazines, newspapers and newsletters appropriate to the art form <u>and</u> to the subject area of your program(s). Subscribe to these periodicals, check them out regularly at a library or media arts center, thumb through them at the newsstand, or borrow them from a friend. Most of the important periodicals appear in my bibliography. Every independent should regularly review AIVF's valuable monthly newsletter *The Independent*. Videoartists should have access to BAVC's *VideoNetworks*. Experimental media artists should be aware of *Afterimage*. Dramatic feature film hopefuls must, of course, read *Variety* or *The Hollywood Reporter,* and *Filmmaker.*

Stay current with the local daily newspaper (and business journal) where you live. Read the entertainment section for information about your peers.

Even more important, read the business section. This part of the paper will cough up more ideas for funding than any other section. Foundations live and die by their investments, and corporations wax and wane with the economy. The business section provides the most current barometer of a community's financial health. I often get funding leads for my clients in this part of the newspaper. Be sure to take an occasional peek at the society column, since it highlights the wealthiest families in every community. For extensive projects, you might start a personal clipping service and file away columns and names for future reference. If the project is very large, then a professional clipping service might be in order.

•**PARTY, PARTY, PARTY:** I cannot overemphasize the importance and usefulness of networking. Get invited to and attend as many parties, conferences and receptions as you can where peers and potential funders might appear. Other filmmakers who are also looking for funds often have the most current information on which funders have just changed their guidelines and who the new program officers are for media grants. Filmmakers on the street actively hustling for donated bucks can possess better and more up-to-date information than a text in a library.

Learn the fine art of **shmoozing**! Get the word out about your current project. Buy people drinks and pry loose as much information as you can! If you keep in mind the principle of the interdependent independent, then you can help lubricate the gears of the information-sharing machine by keeping your friends' projects in mind as well and passing on tid-bits to them even when unsolicited.

SOME MORE SOURCES

• **PBS PROGRAM PRODUCER'S HANDBOOK:** Available for free from PBS (see bibliography). Be sure to request the appendix called "Underwriters of PTV Programming." This lists all the programs that have appeared on PBS for the last ten years along with **all the funders of these programs!** Need I say more?

•YOUR VCR: It is incumbent upon all savvy grant hustlers to religiously check their TV listings. Target any and all programs soon to air that are in any way similar to your own project. The techno gods invented the VCR just so the end credits could be recorded and then played back in slow motion while filmmakers copy down the names of all the funders.

These names should enter the prime candidate list for supporting your own program.

• MONEY FOR FILM AND VIDEO ARTISTS: This book, published by the American Council for the Arts, provides the beginning filmmaker with a good introductory profile of the most obvious and consistent supporters of media as an art form.

Now you know where to get the information you need. It's time to gather and sort through this information so you can put it to maximum use.

RESEARCH

THE RIGHT GRAIN OF SAND

Having access to the tools of research does not guarantee proper use of those tools. This chapter will help clarify and simplify the process of examining available information on funders, the factors for making basic decisions about which funders to approach, and (very importantly) which not to approach.

This process is like sifting sand on the beach. You gather together a large mound of sand and then use a filter that leaves only perfectly sized grains of sand. **Begin with the end in mind.** Not until you know your own program and its goals can basic decisions be made about which funders and funding strategies will be appropriate for each project.

Your research will go through the following phases:

1. Creating an initial list of all potential funders.

2. Paring this list down to a second, shorter, more probable list based on reading individual profiles.

3. Requesting annual reports and guidelines from each funder, and then further paring the list down.

4. Prioritizing this last list, and making personal contact before finalizing your request and writing your grant.

BATTING AVERAGES

As I have mentioned, if you want grants and donations from government, corporate and foundation sources, you have to do some very basic research.

49

Seasoned grantseekers know that this process, though time consuming, helps eliminate many prospects that at first look fine but under scrutiny fail some basic tests. In the long run, good research saves money, time and embarrassment. It means you may decrease the places approached, but increase the rate of success.

Your own rate of success will vary widely depending on:

• The nature and timeliness of the project,

• The range and effectiveness of your research,

• The quality and energy of your personal approach, and

• The strength of the written formal proposal.

Filmmakers often ask about my own batting average. When I did fundraising, I usually received funding for one out of every three proposals submitted. That was because I did not make a formal proposal unless and until the funder gave a very strong signal that the grant would be successful. For every application submitted, there were sometimes as many as a dozen other opportunities dismissed. That means I personally have written over 250 individual proposals that never got funding and researched or contacted over 1,000 agencies to which an application was never sent.

At the other end of the scale, you could employ the shotgun method and earn a batting average of 1-in-250. I moderated a panel recently with two seasoned filmmakers - Theresa Tollini (*Breaking Silence: Stories of Change*) and Peter Miller (*Passin' It On*) - who had separate success rates of 1-in-40 and 1-in-9. Try to be as effective and efficient as possible. Your time and energy are valuable commodities that need to be parcelled out carefully during fundraising so that you still have the wherewithal to make your film.

SUBJECT NOT FORM

As you enter the research stage, begin thinking like a funder. Earlier we discussed the importance of dividing a program into a series of smaller projects. Now is the time to look at how a program can and must dovetail with the interests of a funder.

The vast majority of donors give money to projects not because they are films or videos, but rather despite the fact that they are media. Most foundations have little or no interest in media as an art form. A funder's primary interest lies with the purpose of the foundation and the needs of the community targeted by its board of directors.

Only a small portion of all foundation dollars flows to the arts (including media). The vast majority gets parcelled out to other areas like social services, health, education, the environment, etc. If your research focuses only on media-friendly funders, you will end up with a very small and unproductive list. Experimental filmmakers and videoartists usually have no other choice than to have short lists because of the paucity of sources for this type of work (e.g. The National Endowment for the Arts, a small handful of private foundations and some artists' colonies).

This same rule - subject not form - holds true for all projects involving emerging media that might include film, video or electronic imaging of any sort, as well as videodisc, CD-ROM and multimedia projects as well. Very few funders have an inherent interest in new technologies or new imaging formats per se. On the other hand, if these technologies create effective programs or mechanisms for enhancing the funder's stated purpose and audience, then the producer has a hook.

Before cracking open the resource books examine your full project. List all the possible subject areas you'll be covering that might interest various funders. This list will always contain "Media," "Film" or,

"Video." This list might also contain any of the
following representative headings:

> Arts & culture,
> Children & youth,
> Civic issues,
> Community development,
> Conservation & the environment,
> Criminal/juvenile justice,
> The economically disadvantaged,
> Education,
> The handicapped/disabled community,
> Health care/medical research,
> The humanities,
> International affairs,
> Job training/employment,
> Mental health,
> Minorities,
> Older adults,
> Peace,
> Population,
> Religious programs,
> Social change,
> Social welfare, and
> Women.

A rich and varied topic list can produce a long
and interesting catalog of potential funding possibilities.
Many of these funders may not mention media as a
funding priority. Remember *Stand and Deliver* whose
initial funds came from the National Science Foundation?
Think subject first and form second.

THE SIFTING PROCESS

Using subject headings as a guide, start the process
of listing any and all possible funders. Throw into this
list: any funders recommended by friends and peers,
funders that have a reputation for being generous in
your locale, those that you spotted on credit lists of

other media projects, and funders whose names appear regularly in your press clippings file.

Track down as much information as possible on each before making an approach and an application. Many books include profiles of funders. After reading profiles and making some initial cuts, request annual reports and application guidelines from these remaining funders.

While sifting through these funding guidelines and profiles keep two goals in mind:

1.   To create a short list of highly probable funders that you've researched extensively.

2.   To formulate some intelligent questions that will help get your foot in the door and form the basis of fruitful conversations with each foundation.

WHAT TO LOOK FOR

Through personal contacts and available written information, gather up current details for all of the following items. Keep in mind that any written data may already be out-of-date because of the time-lag between getting and publishing that information. The main categories of research follow:

•**FIELDS OF INTEREST/PURPOSE: The single most important determinant for a successful application lies in the compatibility of a project with the stated interests of a funder.** Find out specifically what a foundation wants to accomplish. Make sure the information is current. If your project deals with health issues and the funder is interested in health, then this may be a good match. You will still need to know more about what kinds of health issues the funder is pursuing. In addition, if a foundation has a stated interest in supporting media, then you have an excellent beginning.

A foundation officer told me that her foundation had listed "environment" as a priority area. She was deluged by applications for films about polluted waterways, recycling and a million other environmental issues. "What the filmmakers did not bother to uncover was that we have a very narrow interest in the environment; we are only interested in tropical rain forests and the issues of sustainability."

• **CONTACT PERSON:** Who is listed as the contact person and who <u>really</u> is the contact person? The two are not always one and the same. For each funder discover:

1.   Who is the head of the foundation?
2.   Who makes the final decision on grants?
3.   Who is an influential program officer or intermediary with whom you must work?

Sooner or later you want to talk to one or perhaps all of these people.

• **GEOGRAPHIC AND PROGRAM LIMITATIONS:** Almost every foundation has a geographic area it prefers or to which it limits its support. BankAmerica only gives to communities where its banks conduct business. Look closely at your project's shooting locations, the cities/states/countries contained in the program's content, and even where distribution will take place. If a funder only supports residents of California and you live in New Jersey, do not waste your time or the funder's time with a proposal.

Watch for limitations in the types of projects supported. A foundation may say, "No funding to media projects," but still be persuaded otherwise. Do not eliminate a funder just yet because they do not like media. If the match between your subject area and a foundation's needs are very strong, then you might overcome this problem.

• FUNDING CYCLE AND DEADLINES:

Foundations present a frustrating environment because so few of them meet to consider proposals on a frequent basis throughout the year. Most look at proposals only three or four times a year. I knew a foundation that met to review proposals only once a year! After discovering the application deadline dates, try to unearth one more crucial bit of information. How does the foundation parcel out its funds during its cycles?

Just because a foundation meets four times a year does not guarantee that it gives out equal amounts at each meeting, nor that any funds have been saved to be awarded during the last meeting of each year. This gives you an excellent gambit for contacting a foundation if all other dooropeners fail. Your question might sound like this: "I noticed that your foundation meets four times a year and that the next meeting is the last one in this cycle. Do you still have funds available for projects or should I wait until the beginning of your next fiscal year to apply?"

• FUNDING STATISTICS: When possible, find either large foundations with healthy fiscal resources, or small-to-medium sized foundations with a strong history of giving to projects like yours.

Gravitate towards foundations that show an openness to new grantees. Find figures for the total number of grants and the total number of first time recipients. Turn this into a fraction, and figure out the odds. A foundation that gave out 500 grants where 250 were new grantees has a 50% degree of approachability. If this same foundation had only five new grantees then your chances would only be 100-to-1, and you might think twice before going there for funds. Some foundations have been set up to support a limited number of organizations over a long period of time. Newcomers have little or no chance to ever squeeze into their list.

Look for two other interesting figures: the total number of applicants vs. the total number of grant recipients. This reveals the full context of competition for dollars and your total odds against winning. Fellowships, for instance, usually have terrible odds: 1-in-20 or 1-in-30 is not unusual.

•INFORMATION AVAILABLE FROM FUNDER:
If you have decided that this is a foundation to approach, request (by phone or in writing) copies of all available information that cannot be obtained in any other way. This might include: an application form and guidelines, their annual report, foundation profile, etc. Read all of this information cover-to-cover before making a formal approach.

• SAMPLE GRANTS AND GRANT RANGES:
Get a feel for the types of projects the funder has supported in the past few years. Find a history of giving to films just like yours, and you may have struck gold. Pay particular attention to what a funder prefers to support (e.g. research, travel, post-production, etc.) and during which part of a project's life the funder likes to enter (beginning, middle or end). Some funders become involved at the beginning of a project and want to be known as first-fund risk takers. Other funders are much more cautious and may only be willing to provide finishing funds or money for distribution efforts.

Look at the dollar amount of each grant for the prior two years. Every foundation has a comfort zone indicated by its average grant range. **During research, discover the specific amount of money that you will target from each and every funder.** Many grants have been lost solely on the basis of the amount of the request. Your request must not be too high <u>or</u> too low for the funder's comfort range. Either scenario can cause rejection of a grant even if the funder likes you and your proposal.

•**OFFICERS AND DIRECTORS:** Become familiar with people in your community whose names appear over and over again on the boards of most funding entities. When a name appears of someone you have met before or someone who is a friend of a friend, then you might be in line for a personal introduction to the foundation. Even when the foundation and the names are not germane to a current project, you are starting the long-term process of knowing who the key players are in the funding world. These are the people who you will try to meet in non-threatening and non-asking situations so that they will be receptive to grant requests in the future.

At this point, you have sifted through a mountain of information and have eliminated a number of prospects. You have created a short, valuable list of probable funders. Can you write the grant now and send it in? No. You have one more crucial and inescapable hurdle to clear - contacting and meeting the funder.

TALK TO ME, BABY

PEOPLE GIVE TO PEOPLE

The whole process of grant making and private donations in America has always bemused me. Why would any organization write out a check (large or small) with very few or no strings attached to a totally unrelated producer? Foundations and individuals in America exhibit a kind of openness and generosity that is hard to find anywhere else in the world.

When funders embark on the path of supporting a filmmaker, they enter into a relationship based on a tremendous dose of trust. Think back on your own charitable giving patterns. To whom and for what reasons have you written checks for charitable causes? Did you give money based solely on an organization's good works, or was it also because someone you knew and respected was involved either with the organization or the request? How has an organization or an individual managed to gain your trust? How many times, unsolicited, did you write out a check to an organization that did not ask you for funds?

Experienced fund seekers fondly spout a couple of aphorisms that filmmakers might take to heart as their own fundraising mantras: "If you don't ask, you will not get," and "People give to people." The only way to get money is to ask. The best way to engender trust in someone once you make the request is to meet them face-to-face.

Statistics for fundraising efforts show that **at least 70% of all grants awarded involved some form of personal contact (by phone or in person).** Any fundraising strategy based solely on written documents is bucking the odds. I began this book by noting that a successful campaign rests on the quality of the project and the quality of the proposer. Once the project is together and quality research has taken place, it is time to get yourself together and begin meeting and talking to funders.

LETTER OF INQUIRY FIRST? NO!

Many funders in their written materials will ask to be approached by submitting an initial letter of inquiry. Foundations love to dangle this red herring in front of filmmakers. Anyone who blithely submits a letter of inquiry prior to making a phone contact has made the task of rejection much too easy for a funder.

Take a moment to imagine and role-play the letter of inquiry scenario. You research the Modest Foundation and discover that your film designed to improve math skills among elementary school children is precisely within the interests of the foundation. The guidelines say "no film or video projects," but you are absolutely convinced that once the foundation hears about the project they will award it funds. The Foundation's literature requests a letter of inquiry before a formal proposal.

You send in a one-page letter. Even though the letter is addressed to the head of the foundation, it is first opened by a receptionist or secretary who has instructions not to pass on any inquiries that mention film or video. The receptionist reads your letter, sees the word "video," and automatically sends a standard rejection letter that precludes a formal proposal or any further contact. You have been cut off at the pass. No well-reasoned project should be rejected this easily.

Whenever possible, make a phone call first and then follow it up with the appropriate written materials. I will be talking about this call very soon. There are instances where a phone call is impossible (e.g. there is no phone number listed), or where a funder absolutely refuses to talk to you until a letter of inquiry is submitted.

In those few instances, you may have no way around this stumbling block.

UP CLOSE AND PERSONAL

A friend of mine once interviewed a foundation head and asked the following question: "How do you like to be approached by filmmakers?" The funder cavalierly answered, "I like to be approached by letter first." Of course this funder likes to be approached by letter first - it makes his job very simple and vastly reduces the filmmaker's chance of getting a fair and full hearing.

The question my friend should have asked was: "What is the most effective way for a filmmaker to approach you and get a grant?" Any honest funder would have to say, "The best way to get support from my foundation is to meet me personally, and then to make a positive personal impression and a compelling case for your program."

I had a meeting once with Susan Silk of the Columbia Foundation. I asked Susan the question my journalist friend should have asked. Her response is well worth noting. **"Well Morrie,"** she said, **"what I look for when I meet the filmmaker is that quality that makes me feel the filmmaker will walk through fire, climb mountains, and swim across oceans if need be to finish and distribute a film."**

Obviously, a filmmaker must meet this funder in order to earn her respect and garner her support. How else can a funder sense your level of total commitment and passion about a project? How better can you gain her trust? Funders know full well that a well-written grant proposal does not always mean an intelligent and committed filmmaker. Anyone can hire a good grantwriter or a good editor.

This is why filmmakers must meet funders personally as often as possible. This also explains why you are always going to have to stay personally involved in fundraising efforts for programs even when working with a team or a hired professional. Another funder once said to me, **"I've noticed that those filmmakers who are persistent about trying to see me, but who are not obnoxious, are the ones who tend to be most successful at getting grants from my foundation."**

Many filmmakers I meet are either afraid to ask for money or are ashamed of having to "beg" for money. You must overcome both of these psychological barriers. Funders are your potential allies. When they give you money, they become your partners and front line advocates. Be proud of presenting this opportunity, and never have the attitude that you are begging for anything. Together you and your supporters will be engaged in struggling for the same cause through your media program.

I HEAR YOU KNOCKIN' BUT YOU CAN'T COME IN

The most effective way to gain access to a funder is to know her personally, or to know someone else who will introduce you. Since most filmmakers do not know any funders, they must resort to an initial phone contact. They hope that the call will lead to a meeting, or at least to an interest in seeing some written materials.

Secretaries and receptionists guard the first gate at most foundations. Enlist them as allies in your search for the right program officer for the project being pitched. If you're lucky, the call will be put right through to the appropriate program officer. In many instances, the receptionist will say "Mr. Y is unavailable right now, would you like to leave a message so he can return your call?"

I try not to offer a message, but if I must, I never leave more than one message. If you want a quick way to antagonize someone leave multiple messages making it clear how upset you are that no one is returning your calls. If funders do not want to talk to you, then even a mountain of messages will not help. If they do want to talk to you, then one message will suffice. Sometimes there is an excellent reason (like sickness or travel) for not getting back to you immediately.

My usual response to a receptionist is: "I am in and out of my office quite a bit and hard to reach. It is much easier for me to call back. What is a good time and day to call and catch Mr. Y?" As soon as possible I try to engage the receptionist in some pleasant small talk. I let the receptionist know something about my project and hope it piques interest in me and my work. A receptionist who has some sympathy for your cause can have a great deal of influence over a program officer actively avoiding your call.

A videographer I know is a genius at this. He once got a receptionist to walk into her superior's office and say, "You are not leaving this building today until you talk to this lovely gentleman who has been trying to reach you on the phone all week!"

THE WINDUP AND THE PITCH

Once you reach the right person at a funding institution, that person may want to know why you are not following their request for a letter of inquiry and what questions could possibly be left that are not covered in their application guidelines.

To establish credibility you must then ask an intelligent question that has not be answered in any written materials. Questions that work can include:

•   "Your guidelines do not say anything about your funding pattern during the year. Do you still have funds available, or should I wait until the beginning of your next fiscal year to apply?"

•   "I noticed in the guidelines that the foundation likes to fund programs with community support. Would individual volunteer support qualify or are you only interested in support from community organizations?"

•   "The foundation's budget guidelines call for a one-to-one match of grant funds, but there is no mention of whether any of that match can be in-kind donations as well as cash."

Hollywood does not present a healthy role model for most aspects of noncommercial media production. But Hollywood does lead the way in helping independent filmmakers with the next key element of an effective approach - the pitch. Quickly, once you have established that you are familiar with the foundation, make a very brief pitch for your project. Here is a fill-in-the-blank template:

"I understand that the Modest Foundation has an interest in [subject area, audience, geography, etc.]. I am considering approaching your foundation for support of a [now summarize subject matter and purpose of your program in under two sentences]. Is this the type of program your foundation might consider for support?"

Keep the pitch short, compelling, and informative. The ball will then rest in the funder's court. If things go well, the program officer will express some initial interest and begin to ask more questions about the project. In this case, see if you can set up a time to meet one another at the foundation office, at a restaurant, or in your edit suite.

Actively and aggressively encourage a meaningful conversation with a funder that will lead you both towards a common goal - the completion of a program that has meaning for you and that helps the funder fulfill the mission of the foundation. Funders are looking for exemplary projects. Foundation program officers want to be known for backing excellent, well-written proposals that meet the foundation's stated purposes and have a high probability of success. All you want to do is help them help themselves by helping you.

Now you can submit any written materials that are requested, including that query letter that I told you not to send earlier. Let the funder take the lead here, and do not press too hard. If a foundation officer makes it clear that there is little or no chance for supporting the project at her foundation, then you will probably not submit a formal application. I say "probably" because I have very occasionally gone ahead and submitted an application to a foundation when the program officer advised against it. I once received $15,000 this way, but only because I had a very strong feeling about the grant and knew that a panel of peers, not the program officer, would be making the final funding decision.

Filmmakers and funders are engaged in a ritual mating dance. Both are looking for a compatible partner. If the dance goes well, both discover everything they need to know about one another. They are still in love and can go to the court house to file the necessary papers.

LAST STOP BEFORE WORD PROCESSING

SOME THEORY

I began this book by postulating something heretical in the funding world - that the formal written proposal is just the tip of the iceberg. I hope the previous chapters have helped convince you of my theory. When a filmmaker finally sits down to prepare the document, much of the groundwork should already have been laid for a friendly reception at the funding agency.

What I have said does not mitigate the importance of creating a perfect formal proposal. The words and figures you are about to write will be entering a highly competitive environment. Even if everything looks perfect, the document will be compared to many other fine proposals. Foundations receive many more worthy program requests than they can possibly fund.

Program officers and trustees enter a meeting inundated by worthy proposals and facing very difficult choices. As a first line of defense, funders begin looking for and then eliminating proposals that have any factual mistakes, financial errors, inconsistencies, blatant omissions or muddled language. They must whittle that large pile down to a manageable size.

The filmmaker's progress now rests on creating a document that clearly and forthrightly makes a strong case for the project. The proposal should also erase any fears a funder might possibly have about providing support. Otherwise, the written proposal may help you lose the grant instead of enabling you to gain the grant.

PREVAILING MYTHS

People who survive by hunting understand that they must learn the prejudices and habits of the animal being pursued. Much of what funders want us to know about their feeding habits can be gleaned from written materials and from conversations. However, as we have already noticed, a subtext underlies conversations and written correspondence between funders and filmmakers.

Why do so many funders harbor so much resistance to the notion of giving money to films and videos? Why does the phrase, "We don't fund media," get stamped on so many guidelines? Before writing a proposal it is sobering to keep a few of these prejudices in mind so that you can begin to erase or attack them in your writing.

- **FILMMAKERS GET RICH.** Funders unfamiliar with independent, noncommercial work immediately think of Hollywood when they encounter the word "media." They may also have heard of a few filmmakers who received grants and who ended up making a lot of money - Michael Moore with *Roger and Me*, or Spike Lee with *She's Gotta Have It* or Ken Burns and *The Civil War*. These filmmakers are the exceptions that prove the rule. Most noncommercial producers will be lucky to pay themselves a bit and break even on a program. This gives filmmakers one more reason to be very detailed and careful about your budgets.

Occasionally a funder will want to preclude the get-rich-quick possibility by insisting that if a project ever earns net profits the foundation must be first on a list for reimbursement up to the amount of the grant. But this is quite rare in the funding world. A filmmaker should, however, be ready to answer a program officer who hints at this notion or asks directly about what happens if you make a profit. The answer could be something like: "Well, in the noncommercial production world, this rarely happens. But if it does I would use the money for additional distribution efforts to underserved populations (or for research and development of my next project, etc.)." In fact, this is where you could cite Michael Moore and Ken Burns as good examples.

• FILMS DO NOT GET COMPLETED. Funders hear horror stories about how long projects take to complete. Somewhere along the line, many funders have gained the impression that projects never get completed. The truth is that almost all funded projects do get done, but they also probably took much longer to produce than the filmmaker first promised.

I worked with a client who was looking for post production support. He received his first grant eight years before we started working together. The filmmaker had promised foundations the total project would take a maximum of three or four years to complete. In the interim, he had not communicated with the foundations, yet he wanted to go back and ask for more support.

Convince funders of your dependability by putting together professional, seasoned crews, by creating a realistic time line, and by creating a solid funding strategy. If the question of completion comes up, then refer the funder to another foundation that has supported a number of productions. Peer-to-peer conversations can be quite persuasive in the funding world.

A funder who supports film regularly told me that in her years of experience only one project did not get completed. I suggested she do filmmakers a great service by calling up every foundation in the country and recounting her positive experiences!

• FILMS THAT GET FINISHED DON'T GET SEEN. Unfortunately, this scenario does happen in the independent production world. Programs get funding, go through post production, and then are never heard from again. Few things are more frustrating for a funder than to back a project and then discover it sitting on a shelf instead of reaching its intended audience. Hence the tremendous emphasis and scrutiny funders give to your distribution plans and your track record for creating work that actually reaches audiences.

• **FILMS COST TOO MUCH.** Yes, as an art form, your production will cost more per minute than other comparable artistic endeavors supported by a foundation. On the other hand, as a tool of communication, your media program may be the most cost-effective mechanism available to a foundation if you consider the total number of people who can be reached, the cost-per-person to reach them through your program, and the longevity of your product.

All of these prejudices share one common element - fear of risk. Be sensitive to the amount and degree of risk that a foundation is willing to endure, and let your proposal help minimize that risk through good, solid writing and planning that addresses every key issue directly.

FISCAL SPONSORS

You need to resolve one more issue before applying for grants. Many foundations and corporations are precluded by law from giving grants to individuals. These funders can only give tax-deductible donations to other non-profit organizations.

Filmmakers have two choices. They can find a non-profit fiscal sponsor, or filmmakers can set up independent non-profit corporations of their own.

For a complete overview of sponsors, I recommend reading *Sponsors: A Guide for Video and Filmmakers* and *Fiscal Sponsorship: 6 Ways to Do It Right* (see bibliography starting on page 109). Theoretically any non-profit agency can serve as a sponsor. Many media arts centers can provide this as a service. Sponsors span a wide spectrum. Some charge a high percentage fee for a number of services, others charge little or nothing but also provide no services except the receipt of your funds.

Pick a sponsor, or sponsors, that you and your funders will trust. Keep in mind that this relationship will become one of the most fundamental toeholds for positioning your project in the public benefit landscape. Some projects have two or three sponsors in order to qualify for grants in different states. Another reason for multiple sponsors is that one sponsor might have limitations on which funders it will let you approach. Try to work with an agency that has a real interest in seeing you succeed and puts few if any limits on where you can apply.

Find one that charges a reasonable fee. Most sponsors are not out to cheat their clients. In fact, some sponsors actually lose money on the arrangement if their staffs become very active in advising and helping out filmmakers. Currently, a fair and available fee rate for a simple sponsorship runs in the 5%-7% range. This is the amount the sponsor deducts from each grant that is processed through their books. Sign a formal letter of agreement **before** beginning your relationship.

For most producers, I recommend the route of using an independent sponsoring organization. However, creating your own non-profit may be a smart move if you:

- Plan to make many large projects over a long period of time.
- Intend to create a substantial on-going organizational support structure.
- Are worried about hefty personal tax liabilities.
- Do not want to lose any percentage of your grants to another entity.

Some books can help with this process but you will still need a lawyer's assistance. Suggested titles include: *To Be or Not to Be* from Volunteer Lawyers for the Arts and *How to Form a Non-Profit Corporation*, by Anthony Mancuso (Nolo Press).

THE WRITER

Your concept and the full understanding of every element of its implementation form the heart of any good written application. This element of preparedness far exceeds the importance of your skill as a writer. If you have decent writing skills, then find a good editor. The editor will review your grammar, punctuation and spelling and also give you feedback on content.

If you do not know how to write, find a professional grantwriter who can be paid on an hourly, daily or flat-rate basis. Lists of writers can be found in the classified sections of media arts center journals or in their membership directories. Foundation Center cooperating libraries often carry a skills bank with resumes on file of grant writers. A professional, however, is not absolutely essential. Anyone on your team, or any friend who has decent writing skills, can collaborate with you to create a compelling document.

Have that person talk with you, while taking extensive notes about every aspect of the project. Filmmakers who work with a writer should pick someone with computer compatibility in both hardware (IBM world versus Apple) and word processing software. The grant will frequently need to be reconfigured and sent off on very short notice. It is a tremendous advantage for both of you to be in the same computer environment.

THE WRITTEN WORD

The written document must strike an interesting and difficult balance between two different worlds - intellect and passion. The writing needs to show that the filmmaker is totally committed to the project and ardent about the subject matter. At the same time, the writing should prove that the filmmaker is a professional who is knowledgeable about the topic and about the craft of creating media.

I have seen proposals take a nose dive because they were slanted too heavily in either of these directions. A proposal with too much emotion and not enough reason will make a funder think you are an untrustworthy nut. By the same token, a totally cerebral and intellectual presentation makes a funder wonder about a filmmaker's motivation and the ability to carry a project through difficult times.

The logic and credibility of your argument will convince the funder the program needs support. The strength of your conviction will compel them to provide support.

Other than this overriding proviso, all the other standard rules of effective writing apply. Use short sentences. Do not obfuscate your points. Remain brief and direct. Use the active as opposed to the passive voice. Lean towards Ernest Hemingway and veer away from Henry James. Repeat after me: **"compelling, convincing, concise."**

Paul Tebbel, Patagonia's environmental-affairs coordinator, provided the following example in an interview in *The Chronicle of Philanthropy* (June 1, 1993).

"I could usually tell by the second or third paragraph whether or not these people were going to get any money," he says. "You know, you get 'Dear Sir: We are a very good environmental organization working on educating the people of our community to be more concerned about what's going on.' Okay. Great. Fine. There's a hundred thousand of those.

"And then you get one that says, 'We're a small grassroots group in Colorado and we have just stopped the Forest Service from completely draining every lake in our wilderness area, and we did it in the following manner: We organized protests, we did sit-ins, we deluged these people with letters. And we have no money but we could really use some to be able to put out a brochure.' Bang! Those people

got money. I mean they showed us what they could do on their own and what they really cared about."

Before firing up the word processor, do one more activity. Look at some actual grant proposals by other filmmakers or by your professional grant writer. Books like this one contain examples. (See "Sample Grant Proposals" section, starting on page 125.) Contact other friends directly for copies of old successful grant proposals, or visit a media arts center to see if it has any on file. If you are applying to the National Endowment for the Humanities, they will send copies of well-written past proposals. Someone else's grant proposal may not provide a template for you, but it will help demystify the process and reduce the fear of writing your own.

THE PROPOSAL

THE WHOLE BALL OF WAX

When you finally get around to writing a proposal for a specific funder, it may be necessary to follow published guideline requirements for content and length or to fill out a special form and budget sheet. Even so, I counsel filmmakers to create a full generic proposal to keep on file and reconfigure as needed.

This proposal will be longer than packets required for most submissions. The advantage to having these materials already finished is that you will have good copy ready for almost any kind of funding situation. It is always easier to edit work down to a smaller size than to lengthen it.

The following all-purpose proposal packet will carry a filmmaker safely through 99% of fundraising situations:

ELEMENTS OF A FULL PROPOSAL

A cover letter followed by:

1. The title page,

2. Table of contents,

3. Introduction/summary,

4. Case statement proving that there is a need for the project,

5. A description of your intended audience,

6. The project's history, including how and why you became involved,

7. A brief treatment (1-2 pages) and, if a dramatic project, a sample scene from the script,

8. Production plans and a time line,

9. Key personnel (brief one-paragraph bios),

10. Distribution plans,

11. Funding strategy,

12. A brief note on evaluation,

13. Budgets (a one-page budget summary, followed by a detailed budget),

14. Miscellaneous supporting materials:

    a. Fiscal sponsor: 501(c)3 IRS letter, a letter of introduction/support, and promotional material that describes the sponsor,

    b. Miscellaneous letters of support for the project,

    c. Press clippings,

    d. Full resumes of all personnel,

    e. Promo reel or work sample.

Most of this material should already be in-hand or in your head by the time you begin to fill in the blanks. Many of the items above are self-explanatory, but let's look at each section in a little more detail.

THE COVER LETTER

Write a one-page letter addressed to the appropriate person at the funding organization. Start off by referring to your recent phone or in-person contact with that person or someone else on staff. Then immediately summarize the nature of the project and how much money is being requested and specifically how the money will be used. There should be room for two more paragraphs in which you will: amplify a bit on the importance of supporting the project, list any other funders who have already given support, and promise to call soon to make sure the packet arrived safely.

This letter may or may not end up getting circulated with your packet. Do not mention anything in the cover letter that is not explained in the formal proposal. Think of the cover letter as a pleasant and personal introduction to what lays ahead for the reader.

THE TITLE PAGE

Aside from the project's title and a brief descriptive blurb, do not forget to put your name (or the name of the key contact person on your team), return address, current phone and fax numbers on this page!

THE TABLE OF CONTENTS

You only need to create this page if the proposal is rather lengthy, say ten pages or more. The table of contents can give the reader a quick and handy way to spotlight specific sections of the proposal or to find the answers to particular questions.

AN INTRODUCTION/SUMMARY

In this section, provide a concise summary of the proposed project including:

> The title (use "w.t." to indicate working title),
> The length,
> Your format (16mm film, 1/2" VHS tape, etc.),
> If it's in color or black & white,
> The type of work (documentary, dramatic, narrative, etc.),
> The subject matter, and
> The intended audience.

Sample:

"*Shaking the Money Tree* will be a 58-minute, color, 16mm Film Documentary that will lead independent American filmmakers safely through the maze of finding donated funds for noncommercial programs."

A CASE STATEMENT PROVING THE NEED FOR THE PROJECT

Write as much in your case statement section as needed to prove that the world must have this program. **This is the most important part of any proposal.** If facts and or figures are available, use them here. Mention and dismiss other programs like yours somewhere in this section. For various funders, you may need to go back into this section and emphasize or expand on those points that are specific to the mission of their foundation.

YOUR INTENDED AUDIENCE

List the targeted audience for your work. If there is more than one audience, prioritize them. Be as specific as possible about the types of people you want to reach.

A BRIEF HISTORY OF PROJECT AND YOUR INVOLVEMENT

Include a very brief note about the reason for and circumstances of your involvement with the project. This personalizes the proposal and provides the background of your commitment. Follow this with notes about what has happened with the project to date (e.g. how much research has taken place, shooting undertaken, etc.).

A TREATMENT

In **no more than two single-spaced pages** write a treatment that whisks the reader from the opening to the closing credits of your program. You can do this in two pages even for a feature-length, dramatic film. Make this writing as visual as possible. Anyone reading it should have the feeling of actually seeing your program in a theater or on a monitor. The treatment lets everyone know what style will be used in shooting, how you will approach your subject, and what the major events are (or are likely to be). Try to capture and convey the personality, temperament and tone of the project.

If you plan to do a cinema verite work where there is no possibility of knowing what will happen in advance - just pretend! The whole idea here is not to give a set-in-stone version of the program, but rather a treatment that accurately represents the message, method and type of program you intend to create. For dramatic narrative work, include a sample scene in order to prove your ability to handle dialogue. If a complete script has been written, then mention its availability and be willing to submit the full script if requested.

PRODUCTION PLANS

Where and when will you undertake production?
What major difficulties, if any, must you overcome
during production (e.g. regarding equipment, personnel,
travel, etc.)? What kind of lifestyle will you and your
crew have to adopt during production and for how
long?

KEY PERSONNEL

Why are you the right person for this job?
Write short, one-paragraph biographies of yourself and
three or four of the most important people on your crew
(Producer, Director, Cinematographer, Scriptwriter,
Editor, Consultant, etc.). These paragraphs should
convince the reader that on the whole the crew is
experienced and knowledgeable in their areas of expertise
and, together, can complete this project with a high
level of professionalism. Beginning or emerging artists
should try to have at least one very experienced person
on the team. If you are including consultants or
advisors, describe how they will be used.

DISTRIBUTION PLANS

Take as much time as needed in this section to
outline all the various ways your program will be
distributed upon completion. Be rigorous and vigorous
in this section. List all your possible markets, and be
sure to place them in an appropriate chronological
sequence (e.g. domestic theatrical, then home video,
then colleges and in what types of classes, etc.). Mention
whether the program will be self-distributed or given to
professional distributors and, again, for which markets.
If you have already spoken with distributors who provided
positive responses, or any usable statistics, list those
here. If you have not talked to a distributor, then go
ahead and list the types and specific names of

distributors you will eventually contact. Let the accumulation of detail in this section prove that you have done the necessary homework on distribution and that the program will have an excellent chance to actually be seen once it is completed.

YOUR FUNDING STRATEGY

Assume that no solitary funder will grant enough money for an entire program budget. From whom, using what rationale, and how will you raise the rest of the money? Usually filmmakers list a combination of projected support from foundations, corporations and individuals. Give the dollar amount or percentage of the budget that you hope will come from each source. Consider including special fundraising events and sales from promotional items (e.g. T-shirts and posters). As you begin to actually get donations, start listing the names of all committed organizational donors in this section. Funders tend to cluster around the support of other funders. Do not give the names of any private individual donors unless they specifically give you permission to use their names in proposals.

EVALUATION

Because funders are accustomed to gauging the success and effectiveness of most projects through some evaluation process, they want to know how your media project will be evaluated. For most media projects the question may seem whimsical. How do you evaluate an experimental film, for instance?

For most filmmakers, evaluation will mean a combination of any or all of the following: examination of critical response, total number of sales in intended markets, anecdotal evidence from peers, focus group opinions, evaluation from users, awards won at festivals, etc. If you are creating a program that intends to make a quantifiable and measurable change in the world, then evaluation should be built into planning. For instance, if you create a series of public service announcements to decrease the number of cigarettes sold in a county in a one-year period, then implement a way to document and count sales.

A TIME LINE

Refer to the earlier section (TIME & MONEY) on creating a time line. The only difference now is that once the project has begun you must start showing how many activities have already been completed and where you currently sit on the time line each time it is sent out.

BUDGETS

Create two budgets for this packet. The first will be a one-page summary of your detailed budget. This gives the reader a quick overview of the full range of projected expenses and subtotals for major categories.

Immediately following this page, attach a full, detailed, complete budget covering all program expenses (including start-up distribution funds) and a projected/actual income summary that illustrates what appeared in the "Funding Strategy" section of the proposal.

It is very important to deal directly with any possible questions or red flags thrown up by any figure. Do this by writing explanatory notes. Write as many as needed for any item that might perplex or confuse a reader.

When Yasha and Carrie Aginsky proposed the film *Toward the Future*, they listed a shooting ratio of 20:1 - an unusually high figure. They knew this might cause problems with funders, so the Aginskys included a note with the budget explaining that they would be in Russia where Kodak film is scarce. In addition, shooting would be cinema-verite style at unstaged, spontaneous events. Now the funder could feel comfortable about the figure without having to call the filmmakers for an explanation.

FISCAL SPONSOR

If you are using a fiscal sponsor then have on file a copy of their IRS letter that proves they received 501(c)3 non-profit status. You may be asked to attach this to proposals. Also have on file a strong letter of commitment and support from the Director of the organization and copies of promotional materials or brochures that describe the organization's mission, activities and history.

LETTERS OF SUPPORT

Support letters are an extremely effective way to shore up the credibility of you and your program and to substantiate any claims that you have embedded in your proposal. As early in the process as possible, begin to request strong letters of support from: professional associations and individual experts in the subject area of your film, distributors, potential users, and well-respected media producers. Make it a habit to gather these letters throughout your life as a professional. When appropriate, attach two or three letters to a proposal. Too many support letters in a proposal tend to diminish the effectiveness of each.

PRESS CLIPPINGS

Keep files of all press coverage including reviews of past work and any feature articles on yourself or key crew members. **Make legible copies, do not reduce**

print size, and use standard 8-1/2 x 11 paper only!
Attach a couple of the most glowing clips to your
proposal unless precluded from doing so by the
application's instructions.

FULL RESUMES OF PERSONNEL

Funders rarely request full resumes, but have
these in your files just in case you need to substantiate
the biographical paragraphs contained in the proposal.
Few things are more frustrating than trying to hunt
down your cinematographer's full resume for tomorrow's
grant deadline when that person is on a shoot in Tibet.

PROMO REEL OR WORK SAMPLE

The sample video has become an increasingly
important and necessary part of fundraising. At the
beginning of a project, you may only be able to show
clips from past work. Once a project has begun, you
will probably need a sample of actual footage in order to
raise the rest of the program budget.

When showing previous work, try selecting a
section similar to the project you are proposing. For
documentarians planning to do more documentaries,
this is simple. However, what if you are a documentarian
who wants to direct a narrative feature? There is no
way out of investing in the creation of a short dramatic
clip that shows you know how to work with actors. The
same holds true for commercial producers who want to
begin making personal noncommercial programs. Do
not submit sample clips from previous corporate videos;
they will not be given serious consideration by funders
and panels that are inundated with requests from
experienced filmmakers who have spent their lives doing
noncommercial work.

A 10 to 12-minute promo clip will suffice for

most purposes. Keep in mind that in many cases the viewer might look at only the first five to six minutes, so place the strongest images up front! Try to create a clip that has no technical problems (with sound or image), and contains gripping, compelling content, eloquent and persuasive dialogue, or events that immediately capture our attention. A mediocre or poor clip will make it difficult for a funder to justify giving you a grant.

Before submitting any clip be sure to ask funders whether or not they will look at a tape and what format is preferred (VHS, 3/4", 16mm, etc.). It is common courtesy to include a stamped, self-addressed return envelope for your tape if you want it back.

Sign the introductory cover letter, place it on top of the proposal (no fancy covers or binding are needed), carefully slip everything into a large envelope, attach some attractive commemorative stamps, and drop it off at your local post office well before the announced deadline.

GOOD HOUSEKEEPING

THE FINE TUNING WINDOW

Just because the grant has been submitted doesn't mean your hustling days are over. There is still an opportunity to do some fine-tuning that can make or break your chances for success.

Call your program officer about ten days to two weeks after submitting the written document. Make sure that this is well before the official panel or Board of Trustees will meet to make its decision. The contact could go something like this: "I'm calling to make sure that my proposal arrived safely and to ask if you have had a chance to look at it yet. Does everything seem in order? Are there any questions I can answer about the proposal?"

A friendly program officer can be extremely helpful at this stage. She can tell you if there are any gross errors or omissions. The program officer can ask you to explain parts of the proposal that may cause difficulty for the Trustees. Often, if the relationship is good, the officer will allow you to give updates on the proposal and submit them before the grant goes to the panel or person who makes the final decision.

After my very first workshop, one of the participants, video/performance artist Susan Banyas, called to tell me this was the most important thing she had learned at the seminar. The day after the workshop she called her contact at a foundation where her proposal for a videotape was pending. The officer said how pleased she was to hear from Banyas. The officer was having difficulty understanding one section of the proposal and was certain this would cause problems with the Trustees. She allowed Banyas to rewrite that portion of the proposal and, sure enough, the grant was awarded.

Even if a rewrite is not allowed, at least the program officer has new details that can be mentioned in person during a panel meeting should questions arise. If, for instance, you suddenly receive some funding from another source, this is great news to give the funder. One of my clients had proposals pending at three foundations simultaneously. Two funders awarded him grants before the third went to panel. He called the foundation to let them know that the film's budget should be changed to reflect two pending grants as "actual" instead of "projected." When his proposal finally went to the panel, his case was suddenly much stronger because two other foundations had applied their seal of approval.

Never assume that funders will contact you about problems they find in a written document. Very few funders have the time or inclination to be proactive in this way. The onus lies on the filmmaker to take charge of the process as much as possible. Maximize opportunities during this short window of opportunity between the date of submission and the time of deliberation.

YOUR JOURNAL

The brain with its myriad of neurons is like a sponge, but it can only absorb and retain so much information. This is why we have the benefit of the written word and why I always keep a journal of each and every contact with a funder.

Whether the journal consists of a three-ring binder or files on your computer is immaterial. Create a separate page or file for each funding entity. Then maintain a list of chronological entries for every interaction with that funder (phone, letter, in-person). Jot down notes about impressions, personal facts you pick up, and follow-up reminders.

Always review this journal page before making your next contact. Quite often it provides some excellent openers to a conversation. In one instance, a funder mentioned to me that her husband collected Cadillac memorabilia. When a member of the Bay Area Video Coalition donated a few posters from the Ant Farm's Cadillac Ranch sculpture, I turned around immediately and sent one to the funder as a thanks for past support! For a sample page from my own journal turn to page 123 of the appendix.

RECORD KEEPING

Once you get serious about looking for funds, the number of grants and proposals being juggled at the same time can get quite confusing. The easiest way to handle this level of detail visually is to create a simple chronological chart of all proposals. The information to keep track of for each project should include: date of the proposal, date of reply, amount of your request, and the nature of the proposal.

RECORD KEEPING PAGE FOR PROJECT X

DATE/AMT. OF APPLCTN	FOUNDATION APPROACHED	PROJECT REQUEST	RESULTS
5/1/93 $40,000	Lotsabucks Film Foundation	Production support	10/1/93 rjctd
5/2/93 $20,000	Megabucks Fund	VHS copies of film to be given free to schools	8/15/93 $10,000 grant!
7/7/93 $6,000	Poorfolks Fund	Tour of Project X to rural communities	(pending)

[etc.]

Keep this record visible in your office at all times. Consult it regularly as a reminder of what grants are outstanding. For positive reinforcement, highlight in yellow, or circle in red all those proposals that are accepted. The only other record keeping device should be a separate manilla file folder for every funder and, over the years, for each application to any funding agency.

CLOSING SCENARIO ONE: CONGRATULATIONS, YOU WIN!

Actually, for smart filmmakers, no real closing scenarios exist in the funding world. Anyone in this game for the long haul considers both acceptance and rejection as parts of an on-going relationship over a number of years.

If you are lucky enough to get an acceptance letter, then do the gracious and proper thing. Call to thank your program officer, and write a short sincere letter of thanks to the director of the funding agency. I have been known to go one step farther and hand deliver a single flower in a simple vase. The rule is not to do anything ostentatious or expensive. A simple "thank you" is often quite enough.

Read the grant acceptance letter or contract very carefully, and arrange to comply with any and all provisions that the funder places on the grant. If they require quarterly updates or a final report, submit the materials on time. Ask the funder if the organization wants to be thanked by name in all your publicity and on the film itself, or if they would rather remain anonymous. Not every funder wants to get public recognition for a gift since it just brings more people like yourself to their doors!

Stay in touch throughout production and post-production. Invariably the project will change somewhat and may end up costing more and taking longer than you had promised the funder in the initial application. Most funders can live with any reasonable change if the filmmaker has maintained regular contact.

Peter Miller in his article "A Fistful of Dollars" (*The Independent,* April 1992), relates a story about Stephanie Black's project, *H-2 Worker.* Black began raising money for her project by showing funders a clip about Mexican migrant farm workers even though she ended up making a documentary on Jamaican sugar cane harvesters in Florida. Black was able to do this because she maintained the original mission and intent of her proposals, even though the specific focus changed, and because she stayed in contact with her funders.

Arrange for as many of your supporters as possible to see the work once it is complete. VHS is so inexpensive that I recommend sending a free cassette copy to anyone who has given a substantial gift (pick any dollar figure that is appropriate for your project). Invite supporters to come to a free public screening at which they will be recognized, or take a copy to the organization and show it in person to staff and trustees during their lunch hour. A little bit of maintenance at this juncture goes a long way towards making funders receptive to your next proposal and to the requests of other filmmakers.

CLOSING SCENARIO TWO: SORRY, YOU LOSE.

Again, do not take a rejection as the end of the line. The principle at this point is to maintain composure and maintain contact. Everyone who looks for grants receives many more rejections than acceptances. Typically these rejections come in a generic form that goes something like this:

"Dear Applicant:

We have given your proposal careful consideration. While we find your project of considerable merit, our trustees are saddened to have to inform you that we cannot provide you with support at this time. The foundation receives many more excellent proposals than it can possibly fund at any one time. We hope you will not take this rejection as a comment on the worthiness of your work. We wish you the best of luck in finding support elsewhere."

Apply a magnifying glass to this typical rejection notice, and you will not discover exactly why the proposal did not get funded. Once you recover from the disappointment and possibly anger of rejection, make a call to the funder. For first-time grantseekers, this is often a difficult call. Be pleasant, and try something like the following:

"I received your rejection notice the other day. Of course I am disappointed, but I understand you cannot fund everyone. I want to thank you for taking the time to seriously consider my request. I just wanted to call and ask, since the letter was very general, if you could tell me a bit more about what happened during the panel meeting and why the project did not get funded? Are there changes you could suggest I make to strengthen my proposal as I go to other funders?"

Make this call every time a funder rejects a proposal. Most government funders are required to maintain notes during panel meetings. These notes, in some form, should be available to a filmmaker upon request. Private foundations and other funders are not required to do this, and they can sometimes be more difficult to approach.

Primarily, the conversation may bring out information that is very important to future proposals elsewhere. Maybe the funder loved the project but was out of funds for this fiscal year and would allow a resubmittal in a few months. Perhaps, as with one of my clients, the panel loved the project idea but hated the videotape work sample submitted with the proposal.

If a program officer is crazy about the project, then now is a perfect moment to ask about "discretionary funds" - pots of money that staff members can give out at their own discretion to projects they like that would not normally meet a funder's published guidelines. This is a good time to solicit suggestions for other appropriate places to approach, although funders do not like to "rat" on one another and invariably say, "Don't tell them I sent you!"

Secondarily, this contact puts funders on-call that the filmmaker is a long-term, serious player in this field. It lets the funders know that each time they reject the filmmaker there will be a polite but firm call for clarification. Let me emphasize "polite."

A filmmaker once said to me, "I tried that call, Morrie, and it didn't work." When I asked for more details he went on to say, "Well, I was very angry when I got my rejection letter so I called the foundation immediately and told them they had made a big mistake and that it was their obligation to fund my proposal since it was so clearly within their guidelines."

This type of attitude will only cause detriment to you, the project, and the proposals of other filmmakers. Do not get mad; get even. Stay in contact with funders who reject you. When your program is completed, send them a press release that lists all the other intelligent funders who were smart enough to lend you support. Then, when the time is right and the project appropriate, come back and ask for support again.

INDIVIDUALS

PRESSING THE FLESH

Going directly to individuals for support has become more popular with filmmakers in the past few years. Many forces have combined to push filmmakers into this arena of fundraising. Foundations, corporations and government sources have "topped out." Their numbers and dollars have remained fairly static during recessionary times while the demand and competition for those limited resources have increased. Filmmakers creating very controversial works find many funders becoming more traditional and conservative. Funders are less willing to take risks that might upset trustees or politicians.

Filmmakers have begun to realize what other non-profits have known for a long time; individuals are an excellent source of support. This money arrives faster than grants and, in many instances, is easier to get. Fundraising from individuals gives filmmakers a proactive way to take control, obtain some quick positive reinforcement, and establish direct contact with supporters. If you are working on a project that is politically sensitive or on a subject that is ahead-of-its-time, then individuals may be the best way to raise money and sidestep the more conservative environment of grants.

Before you stop writing grants and switch completely to individuals, let me mention the downside. Raising money from individuals takes a labor-intensive effort. Most strategies for getting money from individuals will work if done correctly, but the funds often arrive in dribbles with a few large donations here and there. The most attractive aspect of grant writing is that one good proposal to the right place can net a donation of thousands of dollars. With individuals, the checks might cluster in the range of $50 to $100 per donor.

Most projects should explore a healthy mix of grant support from foundations and direct donations from individuals. Although the majority of the projects I see lean heavily towards grants as their primary income, I have known other models that emphasize individual support. For instance, Vivienne Verdon-Roe (who won an Academy Award for *Women - for America, for the World*) has a philosophical commitment to throwing grassroots fundraising parties both as a way to garner many small donations, and also as a consciousness raising and coalition building tool for ending the arms race.

TARGETING

Every film has its constituency, and every filmmaker has friends, acquaintances, relatives and fans. The search for individual donations begins here. Start by mapping out and listing as many individuals as possible who might lend support to your program. Targeting takes three steps:

1. Identify people and places,

2. Qualify these people by the amounts they can afford to give or by their access to specific resources (equipment, space, expertise, other potential supporters, etc.),

3. List the best method of getting support from each and the best person to pursue that method.

Brainstorming is an effective, enjoyable and efficient way to quickly generate this first list. Throw an informal evening get-together where you invite close friends and current or potential future supporters of the project. Provide wine and cheese or dessert, and promise everyone that the meeting will not take more than 90-minutes. Buy a marking pen, put some butcher paper up on a wall for taking notes, and then encourage everyone to start calling out names of people and places that might give money or resources to your film.

Whenever possible, place a dollar amount or specific resource next to each name.

As with foundations, filmmakers need to research the right amount to ask from each individual. It is surprising how public this information is! Many people at the brainstorming session will already know how much an acquaintance or local philanthropist likes to give. If not, then quite often these people donate to other causes and are listed in the brochures of local non-profit art organizations under a specific category of giving.

For each name, select one or more of the following mechanisms as the most appropriate approach:

- The one-on-one, in-person appeal,
- An invitation to a fundraising party, and/or
- A direct mail letter.

ONE-ON-ONE

The idea here is to have an in-person, face-to-face meeting with the potential donor. This could be one-on-one or two-on-one, depending on the size of a project and its team. The meeting might be between just the filmmaker and the donor, or the director and producer and donor.

This direct approach works best with people that you or someone on the crew has already met before in some other context. Begin with a telephone call. Discuss your project with the donor. Ask permission to send information and then arrange for a meeting.

Very occasionally a donor will offer to send a check just as a result of this call. I worked with a filmmaker in Los Angeles who was embarking on a large noncommercial project. She decided to begin fundraising by calling a few wealthy individuals she knew from previous commercial projects. Her very first call resulted in a donation of $20,000! This is rare. It happened because the filmmaker had an established rapport with the donor and her project was about a topic close to his heart - the neighborhood where the donor grew up as a child. He stopped her pitch midway through the phone conversation and said, "Just tell me how much you need, and I'll write you a check." The filmmaker knew how much to ask for because she had researched the amounts this donor typically gave to local charities.

If you do not know the donor well, then a meeting will be in order. The meeting can happen at the studio or edit suite, in a restaurant (be prepared to offer to pay for the meal), or in the donor's home or office. Let the donor pick a convenient location, but an edit suite where you can show some actual footage on a flat bed or VCR is an ideal setting.

Does it take courage to do this kind of fundraising? Yes. Can anybody do it? Yes. You just need to have a great deal of conviction about the project and a persuasive, short appeal. If you are shy and inexperienced, then try role-playing with a friend. Switch roles so you can see how a donor feels as well.

There is a science to making an "ask," but the rhythm of it boils down simply to: a few minutes of polite conversation, a few minutes of explanation about the project, an offer to answer questions or clarify points, and then the request (for money, resources, use of a home for a fundraising party, etc.).

Fundraising professionals are split about whether or not to ask for a specific amount. If you know how much the donor is worth, then I would ask for a specific amount a little bit higher than that donor's average donation. Everyone agrees, however, that **after making the request you should remain absolutely silent and wait for a response, even if the silence seems to go**

on forever. The rule here is that the first person to talk after the request loses!

The donor might say, "But that's a lot of money!" An appropriate response would be "Yes, and that's exactly why I am coming to you" followed again by silence. Individual donors are more likely to be flattered than insulted by a large request. When a filmmaker asks for too little, then donors think either not enough research was done, feel insulted, or jump at a chance to get off the hook for much less than they could really afford.

The donor might say, "No, thanks." In that event, you can offer a polite "Thank you for your time" and move on. If there was some genuine interest, you can try a fall-back position and ask for something else. For instance, if they said no to giving money, then ask to use their home for a fundraising event or the copy machine at their firm to duplicate press packets, etc. If you don't ask, you won't get.

FUNDRAISING PARTIES

By "fundraising party" I do not mean a fundraising benefit event where people pay an admission fee. Simply, this casual evening affair offers potential supporters a chance to come to someone's home and learn about your project. All invited guests are well aware that they will be asked for money, so there is no hidden agenda.

I advise most of my clients to include these parties in their fundraising strategies. The affairs can be arranged rather quickly (six to eight weeks lead time), inexpensively (often the host covers the cost of refreshments and the filmmaker pays for postage/printing), and, if conducted properly, absolutely do raise money. Depending on where the party happens, who shows up, and the urgency of your pitch, the event might bring in $500, $3,000 or $30,000. (These are actual figures from recent events.) As Kim Shelton (*Cowboy Poets*) confided to me, "Our event didn't raise a lot of money, but it was a real morale booster for my crew during a time when grants weren't coming in."

Some key elements make an event like this work. First, you will need to find someone in the community who will offer their home and also provide a long list of friends and acquaintances to invite. Second, you need a very strong eight to ten-minute clip from the program - the kind of clip that grabs people's attention and hearts immediately. The ideal clip will move the audience members so deeply that they will pull out checkbooks and write a donation before the house lights go back up! Third, you must give a strong, heartfelt presentation describing the project and someone else (not the host or hostess) must make a convincing appeal for contributions.

The last element to success in this arena is follow-up. **Except for those people who have specifically asked not to be contacted again, you must call everyone else immediately after the event.** Ask if they have more questions and then request their financial support. Quite often, the majority of donations come not the night of the event, but during the follow-up calls the next few days.

For a detailed primer on how to throw one of these events, turn to the page 157 of the appendix and read the interview with Peter Adair (*Stopping History, The AIDS Show*) who is a master of this fundraising genre, and the detailed materials from Vivienne Verdon-Roe's "fundraising house party" handouts starting on page 164.

IN THE MAIL

Some individual prospects are best contacted by mail. I include in this category people you do not personally know, donors who live far away, and large classes of individuals (members of organizations, readers of certain magazines, etc.) who are most easily contacted by mail.

A direct mail appeal letter should be written in a style that has little to do with the standard grant proposal. In direct mail, "passion" is the key concept. While a grant proposal might try to balance intellect with emotion, direct mail letters go straight for the heart.

There is even some evidence to show that brevity does not help in this arena. In fact, many direct mail guides encourage the writer to lengthen letters by adding a "P.S." every time. The theory goes that the longer a reader's attention is held, the more likely you are to get a donation. Think about that the next time you spend an hour fiddling with all the inserts in a Publisher's Clearing House mailer!

Filmmakers can make use of direct mail in a number of ways. The easiest is a short series of personalized letters to individuals from a qualified list. This letter is usually used when it is the only way you can reach a celebrity or a very wealthy and inaccessible person. It helps tremendously if you can name-drop in this letter, or get someone who knows the addressee to write a note to insert in the envelope.

Even though the odds are long, I have seen these letters work. Bill Kern of Second Type Productions was able to persuade Bill Cosby to donate time to narrate a documentary this way, and Loretta Smith (*Where Did You Get That Woman?*) has received donations from some rock musicians and movie stars through correspondence.

You can also explore the route of mass mailings. Having an excellent mailing list is essential to making this work. Direct mail can be expensive if the filmmaker has to cover all the costs of printing, postage and the purchase of a list. However, with a good list and a persuasive letter, donations will come trickling in.

Paris Poirier and Karen Kiss used direct mail for their documentary *Last Night at Maud's* about the closing of two lesbian bars. They created nine different versions of a letter (one of these is on page 176 of the appendix) and printed a total of 18,000 pieces. Of these, 3,000 were sent to people they knew and to subscribers of lesbian publications. Another 15,000 were used as inserts to a monthly newsletter. Because all the paper and printing were donated, Poirier and Kiss spent a total of only $1,000 (postage and insert fee). The letter brought in a total of $8,500 from 80 different people. The largest donation was $500 from someone totally unknown to the filmmakers.

Was it worth their time? As Kiss puts it, "When all the other fundraising efforts are in a lull you might as well be spending time folding letters and licking stamps! Besides, it gave us tangible, quick results, which was emotionally very encouraging."

Almost every locale has companies and professionals who specialize in direct mail. Try to pick up some free advice from these people or read any one of the many books available on the science of direct mail (see appendix for one of these - *Dear Friend: Mastering the Art of Direct Mail Fund Raising*).

ODDS AND END(S)

BEFORE WE SAY GOODBYE

Before we wrap up this production, there are just a few more areas I'd like to cover. I also have additional anecdotes and some sage advice to share with you.

ESI

If a corporation has its own foundation, then it may be approached in the same way that you would pitch any other private foundation. However, if you are serious about prying loose corporate dollars, then keep the following letters in mind - "ESI." What might be considered unselfish philanthropy in many sectors, becomes transformed into "Enlightened Self Interest" (ESI) in the corporate world.

To get corporate dollars, filmmakers need to pay special attention to pumping up a part of the proposal that we have not discussed before called "Benefit to the Funder." Foundation proposals do not need this spelled out because most private foundations are not primarily concerned with public recognition. As I mentioned earlier, private foundations may even specifically request not to be noted in any publicity.

Corporations, however, are just the opposite. They see their grant as an opportunity to gain more exposure and public goodwill. A successful corporate approach will include a substantial laundry list of what can be gained from supporting your project: billing in all news releases, prominent mention in end credits of the film, placement on the poster and other graphic promotion tools, and public mention at the premiere.

As an example of a value-for-value approach, I like to site the efforts of videoartist Van McElwee. McElwee creates short works that have a relatively small audience and which would seem, at first glance, to be a hard sell to any but a few foundations and funders dedicated to the arts. McElwee wanted to create a new video about temples in India. He had no luck getting a grant for travel from his normal sources so he embarked on a different path.

McElwee estimated the number of people likely to see his work and in how many venues (television, art galleries, museums, university art courses, etc.). He presented this information along with a description of the work he wanted to create to the Government of India and its state-owned airline. Then McElwee said that he needed a round-trip ticket to India along with hotel accommodations and a translator.

The Indian Government engaged in some quick calculations. Out-of-pocket costs would be next to nothing. There is always an empty seat on the airplane to New Delhi, and hotels are inexpensive in India. Many aspiring Indian filmmakers would love to volunteer to follow a seasoned American videoartist around. The Indian officials compared the potential value of exposure on McElwee's tape with their minimal costs for helping him. A deal was struck, McElwee made the trip, and he created a wonderful tape called *Fragments of India*.

Even works with absolutely no commercial potential and a narrow audience can have a whole set of other values that might make them attractive to corporate and business donors. Discover these values and they will lead you to new sources of support in the form of cash, donated goods or services.

SMALL BUSINESS COMMON CENTS

It is rare to get large cash donations from businesses. However, projects that have a strong local angle or that plan shoots in community settings can have success in getting both small cash donations and in-kind support from local businesses.

Zeinabu irene Davis recently shot a narrative film, *Conversation* (working title) in Chicago. Since she also teaches at Northwestern University, Davis made maximum use of her student crew who had many contacts in the local business community. Together they researched a likely list of small business contributors. Phone calls were made and letters sent out asking for donations of specific items from each company. Because of their work, the shoot received many free lunches from restaurants (pizza and fried chicken), as well as the unlimited use of four cellular phones for five days!

Like any courteous and professional filmmaker, Davis has a recognition system in place. Everyone who donates anything to the film receives a personal "thank you" note, a receipt listing the tax-deductible value of the donation, and an invitation to the public screening that will include a program listing all contributors. Any business that provided goods and/or services worth over $500 will also be listed in the end credits directly on the film.

OTHER GUERRILLA TECHNIQUES

Just when I think I have heard every fundraising technique possible a few new wrinkles appear. Who would imagine that the local Rotary Club, Lions' Club or Chamber of Commerce would be fertile ground for the support of independent media? I know of two filmmakers who have been successfully making the rounds as guest luncheon speakers for these organizations.

At these luncheons the filmmaker makes a 20-minute presentation about being an independent filmmaker in America (or a topic of your choice) and then shows a five or ten-minute video sample. The filmmakers invite audience members to come up and talk with them after the lunch to find out more about the project or learn about opportunities for supporting independent work. At that point, you can invite people to become either investors or donors - depending on the project. One filmmaker reported going to 15 luncheons and raising $60,000, and another just did one luncheon and nabbed $1,000. If nothing else, you will get a free lunch!

Tom Ciesielka is an independent producer in Chicago who has been raising money for a one-hour documentary, *Frank Yankovic: America's Polka King*. One of Ciesielka's methods has been to attend polka concerts in the Midwest, especially those featuring performances by Yankovic. Ciesielka stands up before the audience and makes an appeal for support of the videotape, passes a hat, and has plenty of pledge cards available for people to fill out that night or to take home and return later. Ciesielka raises hundreds (not thousands) of dollars at each event. At the same time, he has begun to accrue a qualified mailing list that should generate a number of cassette sales when he goes into home video distribution.

Another filmmaker described how she got a large cash donation from a famous rock star. She was working on a documentary about Vietnam and knew one particular musician who had a great interest in the topic. She also learned that this performer was practically impossible to reach either by phone or by mail. So this intrepid filmmaker did the only thing left to do. She went to every concert the musician was giving on an East Coast tour until she was able to worm her way into his dressing room during an intermission. The filmmaker introduced herself, made a quick pitch for the project, and asked for support. The rock star may have been a little shocked, but he was moved by the pitch and respected the tenacity of the filmmaker. Soon after, the filmmaker received a check for $10,000.

MARKETING WITH INTEGRITY

Emerging and first-time filmmakers must clear the opening hurdle of fundraising by overcoming a lack of recognition and credibility. Well-known, experienced filmmakers have a much easier time getting a funder's initial attention and making a pitch for their next project.

This means, quite simply and directly, that marketing and public relations efforts are inextricably bound with fundraising - especially for anyone new to the field. Think of it this way: You want to gain the ear of a funder. You want to get your foot in the door and have a face-to-face encounter so your project can get its optimum chance for support. Funders are much more likely to take you seriously, and to answer that phone query when they are already aware of you and your work.

If you happen to feel that "marketing" is a dirty word, then just erase it from your vocabulary and call it something else - advocacy, promotion, promulgation or spreading-the-word. Long term successful fundraising strategies will always fold marketing efforts into the plan. What must be achieved is an environment where the filmmaker and the work maintain a high profile among the audiences that might need or want to use the work or lend it support.

Filmmakers can employ many simple, inexpensive devices for keeping themselves in front of funders. Feature articles in magazines and newspapers, for instance, are an excellent way to shore up credibility. I urge all of my clients to send out news releases on a regular basis primarily to funders (past, current and potential) as well as to the press. The news release is an effective nonthreatening, nondemanding way to keep yourself in the consciousness of a funder.

Whenever you have a screening, send invitations out not only to the local mailing list but to funders across the country (or around the globe) who could never attend but should be kept aware of your name and your work. A number of filmmakers involved with large, on-going projects create simple newsletters or one-page "updates." These are sent out every few months just to let organizational and individual funders know about the progress of a project and to keep up enthusiasm.

Other activities that will help you in fundraising include: interviews on radio or television, guest lectures and presentations, participation on grant panels, and attending professional conferences and seminars. This type of marketing strategy does not earn quick results, but it creates a rock-solid foundation for long term survival in this field.

AUF WIEDERSEHEN

The task of writing this book is not nearly as difficult as the challenge that lies before you as a filmmaker with an artistic vision and a price tag.

I try never to shelter my clients from the harsh realities of the funding world. I hope this book has given you an honest portrayal of the challenges ahead and the practical tools needed to succeed. At the same time, once my clients are committed to a path, I try to provide some cheerleading from the sidelines and a bit of inspiration. When you get to that money tree, give it one righteous shake. May the funds be with you!

APPENDIX

BIBLIOGRAPHY OF PUBLICATIONS AND INFORMATION RESOURCES

BOOKS - FUNDRAISING

The Art of Winning Corporate Grants, Howard Hillman. The Vanguard Press.

Catalog of Federal Domestic Assistance. Superintendent of Documents. Washington, DC 20402.

Corporate 500: The Directory of Corporate Philanthropy, Public Management Institute, 358 Brannan, SF, CA 94107.

Dear Friend: Mastering the Art of Direct Mail Fund Raising, Kay Partney Lautman and Henry Goldstein. The Taft Group, 12300 Twinbrook Pkwy, Suite 450, Rockville, MD 20852. (800) 877-8238.

Directory of International Corporate Giving in America, Katherine E. Jankowski, ed. The Taft Group. (800) 877-TAFT.

Environmental Grantmaking Foundations 1992, Environmental Data Research Institute, 797 Elmwood Ave., Rochester, NY 14620-2946.

Financial Aid for Research, Study, Travel and Other Activities Abroad, Schlacter and Weber. Reference Service Press, 1100 Industrial Road, Suite 9, San Carlos, CA 94070.

Fiscal Sponsorship: 6 Ways to Do It Right, Gregory Colvin. San Francisco Study Center, P.O. Box 425646, San Francisco, CA 94142-5646. (800) 484-4173, ext. 1073.

The Foundation Center: <u>Source Book Profile: Film,
Media & Communications, Comsearch Printouts</u>
(available by subject area on microfiche or in print)
<u>National Guide to Funding in Arts & Culture,
Foundation Fundamentals, The Foundation Directory,
Foundation Center's User Friendly Guide, The
Foundation Grants Index Annual</u> and <u>Grants to
Individuals</u>. 79 5th Ave., NYC 10003. (800) 424-9836.

<u>Fundraising for Social Change</u>, Kim Klein. Crain
Books.

<u>Get the Money and Shoot: The DRI Guide to Funding
Documentary Films</u>. DRI, 96 Rumsey Road, Buffalo,
NY 14209. (716) 885-9777.

<u>Grants</u> and <u>Grant Proposals That Have Succeeded</u>,
Virginia White. Plenum, 233 Spring St., NYC 10013,
(800) 221-9369.

<u>Getting Funded: A Complete Guide to Proposal
Writing</u>. PSU, P.O. Box 1491, Portland, OR 97207.

<u>The Grantseekers Guide</u>, Shellow & Stella. National
Network of Grantmakers, 919 No. Michigan Ave.,
Chicago, IL 60611.

<u>The Grass Roots Fundraising Book: How to Raise
Money in Your Community</u>, and <u>Successful
Fundraising</u>, both by Joan Flanagan. Contemporary
Books, Chicago.

<u>Guide to California Foundations</u>, Northern California
Grantmakers. 334 Kearny St., San Francisco, CA
94108. (Similar texts are available in many states
including OR, MO, NY, etc.).

<u>Maximum Gifts by Return Mail: An Expert Tells How
to Write Highly Profitable Fund Raising Letters</u>, R.
Kuniholm. The Taft Group. (800) 877-TAFT.

Money for Film and Video Artists and Money for International Exchange in the Arts, both from American Council for the Arts, One East 53rd St., NYC 10022. (800) 321-4510.

Revolution in the Mailbox, Mal Warwick. Strathmoor Press.

Where the Money Is, H. Bergen. Society for Non-Profit Organizations, 6314 Odana Rd., Suite 1, Madison, WI 53719.

BOOKS - INDEPENDENT FILM/VIDEO

AIVF Guide to Film and Video Distributors and AIVF Guide to International Film and Video Festivals, both by Kathryn Bowser. AIVF, (212) 473-3400.

Alternative Visions: Distributing Independent Media in a Home Video World, Debra Franco. AFI Press. (Order from AIVF, (212) 473-3400).

Bowker's Complete Video Directory, edited by M.K. Reed. R.R. Bowker, NYC. (800) 521-8110.

Dealmaking in the Film and Television Industry, Mark Litwak. Silman-James Press. 1181 Angelo Dr., Beverly Hills, CA 90210. (800) 822-8669.

Doing it Yourself: A Handbook on Independent Film Distribution, ed. by Julia Reichert. AIVF, (212) 473-3400. (New edition, edited by Debra Franco not available as of this publication.)

Film and Video Budgets, Film and Video Financing, Film and Video Marketing, Home Video, all from Michael Wiese Productions, 4354 Laurel Canyon Blvd., Suite 234, Studio City, CA 91604. (800) 379-8808, fax (818) 986-3408.

The Film Industries: Practical Business/Legal Problems in Production, Distribution, and Exhibition, Michael Mayer. Hastings House.

How to Make it in Hollywood, Linda Buzzell. Harper Perennial.

Index to AV Producers and Distributors, Plexus, 143 Old Marlton Pl., Medford, NJ 08055.

Making a Good Script Great, Linda Seger. Samuel French Trade.

The Movie Business Book, second edition, edited by Jason E. Squire, Fireside/Simon & Schuster.

NICEM's Film and Video Finder, Plexus, 143 Old Marlton Pl., Medford, NJ 08055.

The Next Step: Distributing Independent Films and Video. Edited by Morrie Warshawski. Available from AIVF (212) 473-3400.

Off-Hollywood: The Making and Marketing of American Specialty Films, David Rosen and Peter Hamilton. Grove Press.

Producing, Financing and Distributing Film, Baumgarten, Farber & Fleischer. Limelight Editions, NYC.

Super 8 in the Video Age, Brodsky & Treadway. (508) 948-7985.

BOOKLETS AND GUIDES

Benton Foundation Bulletins (Independent Features, Talk Radio, Using Video and Cable Access). Case studies at $5 each: 1710 Rhode Island Ave. NW, 4th Floor, Washington, DC 20036. (202) 857-7829.

The Bottom Line: Funding for Media Arts Organizations, Adams and Goldbard. NAMAC, 655 13th Street., Suite 20, Oakland, CA 94612

Environmental Film Funders Report, The Video Project, 5332 College Ave., #101, Oakland, CA 94618. (510) 655-9050. $7.50 prepaid.

The Guide to Funding for Emerging Artists & Scholars, FREE from President's Committee on the Arts & Humanities, 1100 Pennsylvania Ave. NW, Rm. 526, Washington, DC 20506.

International Guide of Documentary Buyers, Yoland Robeveille, regic 3i, 5 passage Montgallet, 75012 Paris. Phone:(331) 43422068.

National Endowment for the Arts Guide to Programs, Media Arts Program guidelines, and the Annual Report. Information Office, NEA, Washington, DC 20506.

National Endowment for the Humanities Program Announcement and Media Program Guidelines, and Media Log (listing of 800 film, TV, and radio programs supported by NEH). NEH Public Information Office, Washington, DC 20506.

PBS Program Producer's Handbook, PBS, National Programming and Promotion Services, 1320 Braddock Place, Alexandria, VA 22314-1698; or call (703) 739-5450 and leave your name/address on the phone machine. Available free, updated annually. **Be sure to ask specifically for a copy of the list of "Underwriters of PTV Programming,"** (no longer automatically included in the handbook).

Producer's Guide to Public Television Funding. Free from CPB, 901 E St., NW, Washington, DC 20004-2006.

Public Television's Programming Pipeline (see PBS address above). FREE annual overview of series projects for public television currently in stages of development.

Sponsors: A Guide for Video and Filmmakers, Goldman and Green. Center for Arts Information, NYC. Available from AIVF, (212) 473-3400.

Taking it to the Theaters: The Empowerment Project's Guide to Theatrical and Video Self-Distribution of Issue-Oriented Films and Videos, Trent, Peale and Doroshow, 3403 Hwy. 54 W, Chapel Hill, NC 27516. (919) 967-1963.

Writer's Aide Screenplay Contest Packet. 1685 S. Colorado Blvd., #237-B, Denver, CO 80222.

FILM/VIDEO MAGAZINES AND NEWSLETTERS

Afterimage, pub. by Visual Studies Workshop, 31 Prince St., Rochester, NY 14607.

Angles: Women Working in Film & Video, P.O. Box 11916, Milwaukee, WI 53211. (414) 963-8951. Published quarterly.

B&T's Little Film Notebook, (for super 8 fans), IC8FV, P.O. Box 335, Rowley, MA 01969. (508) 948-7985.

Black Film Review, 2025 Eye St., NW, Suite 213, Washington, DC 20003.

Cineaste, 200 Park Ave. S, #1320, New York, NY 10003.

Filmmaker: The Magazine of Independent Film, 132 W. 21st St., 6th Floor, New York, NY 10011-3203.

Foundation News, Council on Foundations, 1828 L St., NW, Washington, DC 20036. Bi-monthly.

The Independent, monthly newsletter of the Association of Independent Video and Filmmakers (AIVF), 625 Broadway, New York, NY 10012.

Media Arts Information Network (MAIN), newsletter of the National Alliance for Media Arts and Culture (NAMAC). NAMAC, Preservation Park, 655 13th St., Suite 201, Oakland, CA 94612.

NVR Reports, newsletter of National Video Resources, 73 Spring St., Suite 606, New York, NY 10012. FREE!!

Release Print, newsletter of Film Arts Foundation, 346 9th St., 2nd Floor, San Francisco, CA 94103.

Screenwrite Now! Magazine. P.O. Box 7, Long Green Pike, Baldwin, MD 21013-0007.

VideoNetworks, newsletter of Bay Area Video Coalition (BAVC), 1111-17th St., San Francisco, CA 94107. **Includes annual "Video Distributors" and "Video Exhibitors" issues.**

VISIONS, quarterly magazine on film/television arts, Boston Center for Arts, 551 Tremont St., Studio 212, Boston, MA 02116.

MISC. PUBLICATIONS

The Business of Art, Lee Caplin. Prentice Hall.

How to Work a Room, Susan Roane. Warner Books.

How to Survive and Prosper as an Artist: Selling Yourself Without Selling Your Soul, Caroll Michels. Henry Holt & Co., NYC.

Not-for-Profit Incorporation Workbook. St. Louis
Volunteer Lawyers & Accountants for the Arts, 3540
Washington, St. Louis, MO 63103.

The Seven Habits of Highly Effective People:
Restoring the Character Ethic, Stephen R. Covey.
Simon & Schuster.

To Be or Not to Be: An Artist's Guide to Not-for-Profit
Incorporation, Volunteer Lawyers for the Arts, 1 E.
53rd St., New York, NY 10022.

INFORMATION SERVICES

AMERICAN FILM AND VIDEO ASSOCIATION.
(800) 358-1834 (fax (708) 823-1561). Computer
searches for programs by titles or subject. Usually $40
flat fee for non-members.

ART ON FILM DATABASE. Inventory of film/video
productions on the visual arts. Fee to individuals and
educational institutions is $35. 980 Madison Ave., NYC
10021. (212) 988-4876.

BASELINE ONLINE SERVICES. An "entertainment
industry" database. NYC. (212) 254-8235, or LA (310)
659-3830.

COPYRIGHT HOTLINE, ASSOCIATION FOR
INFORMATION MEDIA AND EQUIPMENT
(AIME) (800) 444-4203. Free service answering
questions about copyright. P.O. Box 865, Elkader, IA
52043. (319) 245-1361.

DIALOG INFORMATION SERVICES. (800) 334-
2564. On-line database accessible by individuals and
institutions. Used by many libraries and universities.
Contains the Foundation Center databases (Files 26 &
27) and NICEM's A-V Online (File 46).

NICEM EZ CUSTOM SEARCH. (800) 468-3453. Will do customized computer search of its vast databases on films, videos, producers, distributors, filmstrips, etc. $50/hr. + .20/unit.

PBS VIDEOFINDERS. (900) 860-9301. $2/first minute, $1 every minute thereafter. Computer search for film/video programs (by title, subject, filmmaker, etc.) for works on PBS or in R.R. Bowker's guide.

MEDIA ARTS CENTERS

The following organizations provide assistance, workshops and publications for independent (really interdependent) film and video makers. A comprehensive list can be obtained in the National Alliance for Media Arts and Culture's <u>Member directory</u> (address below).

AMERICAN FILM & VIDEO ASSOCIATION
8050 N. Milwaukee Ave.
P.O. Box 48659
Niles, IL 60648
(708) 482-4000

ASIAN CINE VISION
32 E. Broadway
New York, NY 10002
(212) 925-8685

ASSOCIATION OF INDEPENDENT VIDEO AND FILMMAKERS (AIVF)
625 Broadway, 9th Floor
New York, NY 10012
(212) 473-3400

BAY AREA VIDEO COALITION (BAVC)
1111 17th St.
San Francisco, CA 94107
(415) 861-3282

THE BLACK FILMMAKER FOUNDATION
Tribeca Film Center
375 Greenwich St., Suite 600
New York, NY 10013
(212) 941-3944

BOSTON FILM AND VIDEO FOUNDATION
1126 Boylston
Boston, MA 02215
(617) 536-1540

CENTER FOR NEW TELEVISION
1440 N. Dayton
Chicago, IL 60622
(312) 565-1787

FILM ARTS FOUNDATION
346 Ninth St., 2nd Floor
San Francisco, CA 94103
(415) 552-8760

FILM/VIDEO ARTS
817 Broadway
New York, NY 10003
(212) 673-9361

IMAGE FILM/VIDEO CENTER
75 Bennett St. NW, Suite M-1
Atlanta, GA 30309
(404) 352-4225

INDEPENDENT FEATURE PROJECT
132 W. 21st St., 6th Floor
New York, NY 10011
(212) 243-7777

INDEPENDENT FEATURE PROJECT/NORTH
119 N. 4th St., Suite 2020
Minneapolis, MN 55401
(612) 338-0871

INDEPENDENT FEATURE PROJECT/WEST
5550 Wilshire Blvd. #204
Los Angeles, CA 90036
(213) 937-4379

INDEPENDENT MEDIA DISTRIBUTORS
ALLIANCE
c/o Artbase, P.O. Box 2154
St. Paul, MN 55102
(612) 298-0117

INDEPENDENT TELEVISION SERVICE
333 Sibley St., Suite 200
St. Paul, MN 55101
(612) 225-9035

INTERMEDIA ARTS
425 Ontario St. SE
Minneapolis, MN 55414
(612) 627-4444

INTERNATIONAL DOCUMENTARY
ASSOCIATION
1551 S. Robertson Blvd.
Los Angeles, CA 90035
(213) 284-8422

NATIONAL ALLIANCE FOR MEDIA ARTS &
CULTURE (NAMAC)
Preservation Park
655 13th St., Suite 201
Oakland, CA 94612
(415) 451-2717

NATIONAL ASIAN AMERICAN
TELECOMMUNICATIONS ASSOCIATION
346 Ninth St., 2nd Floor
San Francisco, CA 94103
(415) 863-0814

NATIONAL VIDEO RESOURCES
73 Spring St., Suite 606
New York, NY 10012
(212) 274-8080

911
1117 Yale Ave. No.
Seattle, WA 98101
(206) 682-6552

NORTHWEST FILM CENTER
1219 Southwest Park Ave.
Portland, OR 97205
(503) 221-1156

PHILADELPHIA INDEPENDENT FILM/VIDEO
ASSOCIATION
International House
3701 Chestnut St., Philadelphia, PA 19104
(215) 387-5125

PITTSBURGH FILMMAKERS
3712 Forbes Ave.
Pittsburgh, PA 15213
(412) 681-5449

SOUTH CAROLINA ARTS COMMISSION MEDIA
ARTS CENTER
1800 Gervais St.
Columbia, SC 29201
(803) 734-8696

SOUTHWEST ALTERNATE MEDIA PROJECT
(SWAMP)
1519 W. Main
Houston, TX 77006
(713) 522-8592

SQUEAKY WHEEL
372 Connecticut St.
Buffalo, NY 14213
(716) 884-7172

VISUAL COMMUNICATIONS
263 S. Los Angeles St., Suite 307
Los Angeles, CA 90012
(213) 680-4462

FOUNDATION CENTER COOPERATING COLLECTIONS NETWORK

The Foundation Center maintains four main Reference Collections in New York, San Francisco, Cleveland and Washington, DC. In addition, it is associated with many free funding information centers (cooperating collections) located throughout the US. They are excellent places to do basic research on private and public funders. The full list of cooperating libraries is too long to list here. Call the following toll free number for the library nearest you: (800) 424-9836.

The addresses and phone numbers for the four major Foundation Center collections are:

79 Fifth Ave., 8th Floor
New York, NY 10003
(212) 620-4230

312 Sutter St., Rm. 312
San Francisco, CA 94108
(415) 397-0902

1001 Connecticut Ave., NW
Washington, DC 20036
(202) 331-1400

Kent H. Smith Library
1422 Euclid, Suite 1356
Cleveland, OH 44115
(216) 861-1933

SAMPLE GRANT JOURNAL PAGE

The following is a slightly edited page from my grant journal. I have changed names to protect the innocent. I maintain a page like this in a three-ring binder on every funder. Using a card file or computer memo are other methods for keeping these records.

**MODEST
CHARITABLE TRUST**
P.O. Box 75444
San Anselmo, CA 94732
(415) 935-5555
Contact: Astoria Oak, Dir. of Art Programs

2/16/92:   Talked to Astoria Oak about "Project X." She says they are already heavily committed to film this year. Isn't too hopeful about my chances but agrees to meet me for lunch on 2/29.

2/29/92:   Lunch with Astoria at Pickle Palace. (She likes jogging, was raised in Midwest, ex-husband 18th Century scholar). We got along very well, but she has no interest in "Project X" and they are out of money for film projects now anyway. BUT, she did say if I ever get in a position where I have a number of other funders and I am short just a bit, she might be able to throw in the difference through discretionary funds.

5/1/92:   Called Astoria to let her know I raised $75,000 and just need $5,000 more. She suggests I send her full packet/proposal and I'll hear in two weeks. (Sent packet that afternoon.)

5/16/92:   Called Astoria to find out "what's up." She says call again in two weeks.

5/26/92:   Yes! Got grant for $5,000! Check will come in two weeks. Astoria asks that Modest Charitable Trust receive recognition in all publicity and on the film itself.

5/27/92:   Sent "thank you" note to President of the Foundation and hand-delivered one orchid in bud vase to Astoria, who was surprised.

6/5/92:   Received and cashed check.

10/5/92:   Called A. to let her know how film was coming along.

1/1/93:   Invited Astoria to Premiere of film at Bijoux and offered free tickets to everyone at the Foundation, but she insists on buying tickets.

2/1/93:   Sent final report and VHS copy of film to Foundation.

4/1/93:   Called Astoria to ask about funding "Return of Project X" and she sounded very interested.

Toward the Future

A Film of Soviet and American Youth-to-Youth Diplomacy

by
Aginsky Productions
3704 Folsom Street
San Francisco, CA 94110
(415) 648-9433

Toward the Future
A Film of Soviet and American
Youth-to-Youth Diplomacy

Every breeze wafts intelligence from country to country, every wave rolls it and gives it forth, and all in turn receive it. There is a vast commerce of ideas, there are marts and exchanges for intellectual discoveries, and a wonderful fellowship of those individual intelligences which make up the minds and opinions of the age.

— Daniel Webster

It isn't enough to talk about peace; one must believe in it. And it isn't enough to believe in it; one must work at it.

— Eleanor Roosevelt

Introduction

Envision a world marked by a fellowship of individual intelligences; a world wherein the most powerful economic, cultural, and political leaders interact and communicate with one another through a firm lattice of friendship and acquaintance that has already been established during their teens and twenties.

Toward the Future will be a ninety-minute, color, 16-mm documentary that will examine the beginnings of just such a latticework. The film will follow a group of American high school and college students as they tour the Soviet Union culminating in a week living with Soviet students and their families in Tbilisi, the capital of the Republic of Georgia. Toward the Future is the first in a projected trio of works examining the Soviet Union intended for theatrical, public broadcast, and educational distribution.

Rarely has there appeared so favorable a moment for meaningful interaction between Soviet and American youth. The current Soviet commitment to glasnost and perestroika (openness and restructuring) has created an unusual window of opportunity to deepen and widen areas of communication and trust. The filmmakers will seize this rare chance to create an important new work that will help the people of both nations discard inaccurate and destructive stereotypes and further their understanding of one another on a people-to-people level.

Toward the Future will explore the many factors that can heighten the potential for constructive cooperation between youth of diverse backgrounds. It will help initiate and document the cooperative efforts of a unique coalition of groups: Sovinfilm (Moscow); Dialogue for Peace, Understanding, and Friendship (Sacramento); Case Western Reserve University (Cleveland); Center for Experimental Education (Tbilisi); and Aginsky Films (San Francisco). Together they will embark on a journey to transcend the barriers between nations, races, professions, religions, disciplines, cultures, and geo-

126

graphic distance — all in an effort to locate, highlight, and illuminate the life-giving forces inherent in charting a cooperative existence.

The Project

In the summer of 1988 a group of highly motivated American high school and college students from Sacramento will travel to the USSR as part of a new educational program, Dialogue for Peace, Understanding, and Friendship. Led by educator Betty Staley, they will embark on an exciting month-long journey of sharing and discovery that will introduce them to university students, young professionals, technocrats, and artists who are likely to be their counterparts during the coming decades.

For the first three weeks they will be in contact with Russian youth in Moscow, Leningrad, Novgorod, Odessa, and Samarkand. The film will focus on the students' experiences as they discover a new culture and explore a new geography. The camera will follow them as they work on a collective farm, prepare meals together, hike to historical sites, visit treatment centers for youth with problems, and attend American and Soviet films.

The students will engage in dynamic discussion groups throughout their journey. They will be extensively prepared for these meetings by Dr. David L. Cooperrider, Co-Director of the Department of Organizational Behavior at Case Western Reserve, who will also accompany the group. Dr. Cooperrider will head a team that will create an important adjunct to the film by conducting a special project funded by his university to document the project in its entirety, provide consultation around the project, and conduct a study of the project's long-term impact (ten to fifteen years).

Meetings and discussion sessions will be designed to generate increased understanding and apprecia-tion for differences between students and their cultures, and to lay the groundwork for new alliances. Students will also share with each other their creative skills in dance, poetry, music, painting, and theater — communicating through the universal language of art.

Their final week in Russia will be spent in Tbilisi. There each student will have the rare and rewarding experience of living directly with Russian families whose children attend the renowned Center for Experimental Education directed by Shalva Alexandrovich Amanashvili. Amanashvili is a Georgian teacher and psychologist who has been acclaimed internationally for his years of work developing a form of education that allows children to become creative, free-thinking individuals.

His American counterpart, Betty Staley, has devoted her life to imbuing adolescents with a significant appreciation for human diversity joined with a sense of responsibility for the Earth and its inhabitants. The meeting of these two educators and their students to share their concerns, hopes, and dreams for the future forms the central fulcrum of the film.

The filmmakers will employ a cinema vérité style to lend to each frame of the film a sense of immediacy and directness. The viewer will experience, along with the students and their guides, the excitement and joy of exploring a new terrain and of engaging directly with their counterparts in a different culture. The groundwork for the film has already been laid by Carrie Aginsky during a trip to the Soviet Union in the summer of 1987 when she met with many of the principals who will appear in the film.

Toward the Future will differ substantially from any other film on Soviet-American relations. Dmitri Devyatkin's videotape *The People Speak* includes a number of stand-up interviews and testimonials by Soviet citizens, but presents very few youth and virtually no interaction between the two cultures. The same holds true for the British series *Comrades* and Robert Gilner's *Russia: Off the Record*. A recent WGBH "Frontline" program did include Soviet and American youth. However, it was severely limited by remaining in the static environment of a studio and relying solely on a debate format.

There have been other excellent works in the areas of cultural cross-fertilization (e.g. *Mao to Mozart* and *Saxophone Diplomacy*) as well as broad political overviews (e.g. Bill Jersey's *First 50 Years of Soviet American Diplomacy* and *Faces of the Enemy*). Where Toward the Future differs from all other previous work is in its commitment to bringing together American and Soviet youth as they discover and meet in natural settings conducive to free and open exchange unfettered by the restraints of program format or space.

As Mary Seton-Watson points out in her essay "The Soviet Way of Life":

> When the Soviet writer Mikhail Roschchin recently asked his twelve-year-old son what his friends at school thought about America, the boy replied: "Americans are fine, but why do they want to drop a bomb on us?" And Roschchin remembered that he once asked an American schoolgirl a similar question about the Russians, and got a similar answer. An increase in tourism in both directions may be the best way to remove such dangerous illusions from both children's and adults' minds.

Distribution

The filmmakers will explore an aggressive and professional marketing and distribution strategy to ensure that Toward the Future receives wide recognition and is seen by as many individuals as possible. Plans include:

- Submission of the film to key festivals nationally and internationally (e.g. New York Film Festival, Berlin Film Festival, American Film and Video Festival, U.S. Film Festival, Moscow International Film Fest, etc.);
- Transfer of the film to 35 mm for limited theatrical distribution in those markets that have traditionally been supportive of independently produced documentaries and where there are populations interested in the subject matter of the film (Seattle, San Francisco, New York, Portland, Boston, etc.);
- A special joint World Premiere theatrical run in local theaters in Sacramento and Tbilisi, the homes of many of the participants in the film;
- Offering the film to the Public Broadcasting System for national airing, and to individual PBS affiliates nationwide;
- Distribution in both film and video to the educational market in the U.S. accompanied by a comprehensive study guide (especially to institutions and instructors with an interest in the Soviet Union, international relations, sociology, peace issues, or youth-to-youth diplomacy);
- International distribution through both theatrical and broadcast mediums;
- Home video distribution to individuals and institutions on a limited scale through direct mail to target markets.

A number of distributors and broadcasters have already expressed a keen interest in being associated with Toward the Future. They include: Landmark Films (San Francisco), Direct Cinema Ltd. (Los Angeles), Altschul Group (Illinois), Jane Balfour Films (London), KQED, KCET, and WGBH. In addition, the key personnel in Toward the Future will make every effort to tour with the film and make personal presentations in public settings to help with promotional efforts.

Key Personnel

CARRIE AGINSKY, CO-PRODUCER–DIRECTOR–STILL PHOTOGRAPHER, and YASHA AGINSKY, CO-PRODUCER–PRODUCTION MANAGER–EDITOR, have been making educational, documentary, and experimental films and videotapes together since 1967. Their credits include: *Putting up the Pickles*, a film about a European-style traveling circus; *Les Blues de Balfa* and *Cajun Visits*, two films about French-speaking Americans and their music; and *Homemade American Music*, a film about American traditional music. Their works have won numerous awards at the American Film Festival, Cine International Film Festival, San Francisco International Film Festival, and World Music Film Festival and have been broadcast internationally on television throughout the United States, England, France, The Netherlands, Denmark, Sweden, Finland, Norway, Australia, and Canada. Yasha Aginsky has also worked as an independent editor on many award-winning documentary and fictional films including *The Hero's Journey, The Word of Joseph Campbell*, and *Las Madres de la Plaza de Mayo*.

STEPHEN LIGHTHILL, CAMERA, has a long and distinguished career as a cinematographer of the first calibre. He has participated in the creation of many award-winning documentaries including *The Day after Trinity, Seeing Red, Gimme Shelter, Putting up the Pickles* (with Carrie and Yasha Aginsky), and *Running Fence*. His distinguished career encompasses work with *CBS Reports, 60 Minutes, CBS Evening News* with Walter Cronkite, as well as Resource Cinematographer with Sundance Institute.

NELSON STOLL, SOUND, brings twenty years of dramatic, documentary, and commercial film experience to this project. His long list of professional audio credits include *Eye on the Sparrow; Date with an Angel; Vietnam, a Television History; Tai Pan; Running Fence; Weeds; Outskirts of Hope; Hopi: Songs of Fourth World*; and many others including *Putting up the Pickles* with Carrie and Yasha Aginsky.

BETTY STALEY, EDUCATOR, organized the youth-to-youth diplomacy project and founded the educational program Dialogue for Peace, Understanding, and Friendship. Staley is a widely respected lecturer on adolescent education, author of the children's book *Ow and the Crystal Clear*, and co-author of *Ariadne's Awakening*. She has taught Russian literature on the high school level for more than fourteen years and currently serves on the faculty of the Rudolf Steiner College in Sacramento where she is Director of High School Teacher Training and teaches history and literature at the Sacramento Waldorf High School.

DR. DAVID L. COOPERRIDER, EDUCATOR, holds the post of Co-Director of the Social Innovations Project and Assistant Professor of Organizational Behavior at the prestigious Weatherhead School of Management at Case Western Reserve University where he also received his Ph.D. Dr. Cooperrider has published widely, including two books — *The Functioning of Executive Power* and *The Functioning of Executive Integrity*. He is currently conducting research on trans-international voluntary organizations and is a consultant to many health care organizations.

DR. WILLIAM A. PASMORE, EDUCATOR, serves as Co-Director of the Social Innovations Project along with Dr. Cooperrider, and is Associate Professor of the Department of Organizational Behavior at Case Western Reserve's Weatherhead School of Management. Dr. Pasmore received his Ph.D. in Administrative Sciences at Purdue University. He has taught at Stanford and Purdue, and served as Visiting Professor at institutions in France and Belgium. The author of numerous articles, book reviews, technical reports, and books (including the three-volume *Research in Organizational Change and Development*), Dr. Pasmore has also received grants for research from Polaroid, American Red Cross, and General Electric.

Brief Treatment

The film begins at the San Francisco International Airport where a group of high school and college age youth make last-minute preparations for their trip to the Soviet Union. An animated and self-assured Betty Staley, teacher, busily briefs the students and their parents at the airport, telling jokes to help ease tensions before boarding their flight. The film follows the group on the plane en route as they practice their Russian and examine maps charting their itinerary. It is at this point that we get to know who these young people are and what their expectations, hopes, and dreams are for this trip. We focus especially on three or four of the students who we will follow throughout the film.

The students arrive in Moscow, a sprawling capital city filled with huge grey government buildings enlivened by banners with slogans proclaiming glasnost and perestroika. Through a series of quick cuts, the film follows the youths on their three-week whirlwind tour of Moscow, Leningrad, Novgorod, Odessa, and Samarkand. Along the way they: receive their first immersion in Soviet culture at a performance of the Bolshoi; work on a collective farm in Samarkand; engage in frank evening discussion sessions with their young counterparts in all walks of Soviet life; sample Russian staples like kasha (buckwheat porridge) and salads with smoked fish; and meet with ecologists, writers, teachers, artists, scientists, and social workers. Everywhere they travel, "Peace!" is the first toast.

Next the film takes us to the beautiful and historically rich city of Tbilisi surrounded by towering mountains and winding valleys. This is where the students will spend their last full week and where the bulk of the film will take place. The film crew has come early and gives us glimpses of life at the Center for Experimental Education. Shalva Alexandrovich Amanashvili and his students are anxiously making their final plans for the arrival of the American students. As in San Francisco, the film focuses on three or four Russian students and their families.

The American students arrive and are welcomed with open arms by their new Russian friends and their families who have agreed to adopt them into their homes during their stay. Amanashvili and Staley greet each other warmly for the first time, he in English and she in Russian. After many months of long distance planning and correspondence, they now have much to talk about in person.

The camera follows the Americans as they settle in and get to know their hosts and Tbilisi. The camera goes with them: up the cable car to Mount Mtatsminda for a panoramic view of the countryside, for a visit to the huge aluminum statue of "Deda-Kalaki" (Mother of the Town), to the Museum of Local History, and to a Russian Drama Theater Company performance of Shakespeare's *Hamlet*.

Around tables on the terrace of outdoor cafés the students discover mutual passions for poetry, art, drama, and music. The Americans have brought gifts of baseballs, bats, mitts, gloves, caps, and attempt to teach their friends the pleasures and intricacies of America's national sport. This sequence will allow for disarming humor on all sides. We will see the students enjoying each other's pop music, trading dance styles and fashions. The film will enter Georgian homes and capture the daily routine of Russian domestic life. We see the Americans helping out in the kitchen with the preparation of traditional Georgian dishes.

As a result of these shared experiences drawing the students closer together, there will be many opportunities for group and family discussions. It is during these discussions that the youths themselves will pose many of the questions of interest to Americans, including:

"How is glasnost affecting communications within the USSR and with the rest of the world?"

"How can we understand what happens when people regard each other as enemies?"

"How is the world different today from the world of our parents?"

"What is the task of our generation? How can we address this?"

"How do you imagine your life and what you will be doing in the year 2000?"

"How can we help each other accomplish these goals?"

The week in Tbilisi comes all too quickly to a close as new friends bid each other farewell, exchange addresses and good-bye gifts, and pose for one last group photo. As the final credits roll over this still photograph, the film ends with a positive statement about what is possible to accomplish toward the goal of achieving world peace through mutual understanding. Through direct experience of each other, Americans and Soviets have broken through stereotypes and differences that separated them and built the framework for mutual trust and confidence needed to create a hopeful future for all.

Toward the Future
Production Schedule
Time Line

Toward the Future will be filmed on location in California and in the Soviet Union between June 25 through August 1, 1988. Processing and printing of the picture and transcription, translation, transfer, and synching-up of the sound will take place in San Francisco in August and September. Editing will begin in October and end with a sound mix in April, 1989. The film will be printed in May and released in June, 1989.

```
1988
January         February        March           April           May             June
pre-production ------------------------------------------------------------------>production


July            August          September       October         November        December
production --------------------->post-production ------------------------------------->
                lab-work --------------------->edit ------------------------------->
                transfer --------------------->|


1989
January         February        March           April           May             June
post-production ------------------------------------------------------------------>release
edit ------------------------>sound cut ------->sound mix ------->printing --------->distribution
                titles ------------->neg. cut ---------->publicity
```

Toward the Future
Budget Summary

16 mm color • 90-minute documentary
shooting ratio 20:1

	cash/in-kind received	total
I Pre-Production • 6 months		
Personnel	$6,000	$41,000
Research and Development Travel	$4,000	$7,500
Materials and Services	$3,000	$9,000
Pre-Production subtotals	*$13,000*	*$57,500*
II Production • 32 days		
Personnel Crew of 8	$14,600	$86,600
Equipment	$7,400	$26,600
Travel (includes per diem)		$42,000
Materials	$400	$12,600
Production subtotals	*$22,400*	*$168,800*
III Post-Production • 6 months		
Services and Related Materials	$12,674	$73,313
Personnel • 25 weeks		$86,000
Miscellaneous		$6,000
Post-Production subtotals	*$12,674*	*$165,313*
IV Distribution • 6 months		
Personnel		$36,000
Services and Related Materials	$3,840	$17,468
Promotion		$3,000
Miscellaneous		$4,000
Distribution subtotals	*$3,840*	*$58,468*
V Final Miscellaneous		
Administration • 18 months		
Personnel		$28,656
Overhead		$18,000
Legal Fees		$6,000
Miscellaneous subtotals		*$52,656*
Insurance @ 10 %		$50,000
Film Arts Foundation, Fiscal agent @ 5%		$25,000
BUDGET TOTAL	**$51,914**	**$577,737**

TOWARD THE FUTURE:BUDGET
16 mm color - 90 min. documentary
shooting ratio: 20:1*

	CASH RECEIVED	IN KIND CONTRIB.	CASH NEEDED	TOTAL
I. PRE PRODUCTION - 6 months				
<u>Personnel</u>				
Co-Producer/Director @ $2,000/mo.	$2,500		$9,500	$12,000
Co-Producer/Production Mgr. @ $2,000/mo.	$2,500		$9,500	$12,000
Writer/Researcher 200 hrs. @$35/hr.	$1,000		$6,000	$7,000
Consulting fees (5) @ $2,000 each			$10,000	$10,000
<u>Research and Development</u>				
<u>Travel</u>:				
1 person to USSR (1987)	$4,000			$4,000
Transportation: N.Y.C., D.C., Amhurst, Clev. (1988)			$1,900	$1,900
20 days Per Diem @ $80/day (1988)			$1,600	$1,600
<u>Materials and Services</u>:				
Preparation Fundraising Film:				
Direction, cinematography, editing, film stock, processing, video transfer, video copies, etc.	$3,000			$3,000
Miscellaneous			$6,000	$6,000
PRE-PRODUCTION SUB TOTAL	$13,000	$00,000	$44,500	$57,500

PAGE 2

TOWARD THE FUTURE: BUDGET

	CASH RECEIVED	IN KIND CONTRIB.	CASH NEEDED	TOTAL
II. PRODUCTION — 32 days (includes per diem)				
Personnel (Crew):				
Executive Producer			$10,000	$10,000
Co-Producer/Director/Still Photographer			$10,000	$10,000
Co-Producer/Production Manager			$10,000	$10,000
Camera operator @ $600/day		$4,200	$15,000	$19,200
Camera Asst./Still Photographer @ $$300/day		$1,600	$8,000	$9,600
Sound Recording @ $400/day		$2,800	$10,000	$12,800
Sound Asst./Grip/Translator @ $250/day		$3,000	$5,000	$8,000
Continuity/Research/Translator @ $250/day		$3,000	$5,000	$8,000
Equipment:				
Camera Package @ $500/day		$6,000	$10,000	$16,000
Sound Package @ $200/day		$1,400	$5,000	$6,400
Still Photo Package @ $100/day			$3,200	$3,200
Misc. supplies			$1,000	$1,000
Travel: 8 people S.F./Moscow/S.F. @ $4,000				
intourist accommodations and air travel in USSR			$32,000	$32,000
local car/bus/truck rental			$8,000	$8,000
Equipment (travel) insurance			$2,000	$2,000
Materials:				
Film: 60,000 Ft. Kodak 7291;7294 negative				
- 150 rolls @ $70/roll			$10,500	$10,500
Recording tape - 35 hours			$600	$600
still film 35mm		$400	$1,100	$1,500
PRODUCTION SUB TOTAL	$00,000	$22,400	$146,400	$168,800

135

TOWARD THE FUTURE:BUDGET

	CASH RECEIVED	IN KIND CONTRIB.	CASH NEEDED	TOTAL
III. POST PRODUCTION – 6 months:				
<u>Services and related materials</u>:				
Develop 60,000 ft. @ .124 per ft.		$2,280	$5,220	$7,500
Workprint @ .205 per ft.		$3,720	$8,580	$12,300
Sound transfer and resolution (35 hrs.=75,600 ft.)				
– @ .075 per ft.			$5,438	$5,438
Edge coding: picture – 60,000 ft.				
+ sound – 75,000 ft.= 135,000 ft. @ .0125/ft.			$1,688	$1,688
Optcals and titles, design			$1,000	$1,000
– execution			$2,000	$2,000
Sound mix: 60 hrs. @ $275/hr.		$5,000	$11,500	$16,500
8,500 ft. of 35mm full coat stock @ $.07/ft.			$600	$600
3,400 ft. of 16mm stock @ $.04/ft.			$136	$136
Full coat rental			$300	$300
Printing optical sound negative – 3,345 ft. @ $.38/ft.			$1,272	$1,272
1st answer print @ $.945/ft.		$150	$3,012	$3,162
2nd answer print @ $.31/ft.			$1,037	$1,037
Master positive @ $.85/ft.			$2,844	$2,844
Duplicate negative @ $.73/ft.			$2,442	$2,442
Check print @ $.33/ft.		$234	$870	$1,104
Release prints: 10 @ $.158/ft.		$1,290	$4,000	$5,290
Still film developing				
– printing				
Archival research and aquisition			$9,000	$9,000
Music composition			$5,000	$5,000
Sound effects research and transfer			$2,000	$2,000
<u>Personnel</u>: – 25 weeks				
Co-Producer/Director @ $500/wk.			$12,500	$12,500
Co-Producer/Chief editor @ $1,200/wk.			$30,000	$30,000
Assistant editor @ $800/wk.			$20,000	$20,000
Apprentice editor @ $300/wk.			$7,500	$7,500
Transcriber/translator			$10,000	$10,000
Miscellaneous			$6,000	$6,000
POST PRODUCTION SUB TOTAL	$00,000	$12,674	$152,667	$165,313

PAGE 4

TOWARD THE FUTURE: BUDGET

	CASH RECEIVED	IN KIND CONTRIB.	CASH NEEDED	TOTAL
IV. DISTRIBUTION — 6 months:				
<u>Personnel</u>:				
Executive producer @ $2000/mo.			$12,000	$12,000
Co-Producer/Director @ $2000/mo.			$12,000	$12,000
Co-Producer/Business Manager @ $2000/mo.			$12,000	$12,000
<u>Services and Related Materials</u>:				
Video transfer (off inter-positive)				
- 8 hrs. @ $350/hr.		$640	$2,160	$2,800
stock 90 min. @ $2.50/min.			$225	$225
1 in. master 90 min. @ $325/hr.			$490	$490
10 - 3/4 in. dubs @ $80 ea.		$200	$600	$800
Blow-up to 35mm: interformat and 10 prints:				
1st print @ $.50/ft.			$1,673	$1,673
2 - 10 prints @ $.215/ft.= $720 ea.			$6,480	$6,480
35mm film stock for Soviet use		$3,000		$3,000
<u>Promotion</u>:				
Festivals			$1,000	$1,000
Advertising			$2,000	$2,000
<u>Miscellaneous</u>:				
Study guides - (writing and printing)			$4,000	$4,000
POST PRODUCTION SUB TOTAL	$00,000	$3,840	$54,628	$158,468

TOWARD THE FUTURE:BUDGET

	CASH RECEIVED	IN KIND CONTRIB.	CASH NEEDED	TOTAL
V. FINAL MISCELLANEOUS:				
Administration for Project (18 mos.)				
Personnel:				
Secretary/Business Mgr. @$1,000/mo.			$18,000	$18,000
Bookkeeper 16 hrs./mo. @ $12/hr.			$3,456	$3,456
Acct. 2 days/mo. @ $25/hr.			$7,200	$7,200
Overhead: $1,000/mo.				
Office rental, telephone, telex, postage,				
copies, supplies, translation (Russian/Georgian)			$18,000	$18,000
Legal Fees:			$6,000	$6,000
FINAL MISCELLANEOUS SUB TOTAL	$00,000	$00,000	$52,656	$52,656
Case Western Reserve University:				
Research Design and Documentation				
(10 - 15 year study)				
(Separate budget)				
Insurance @ 10% of final budget			$50,000	$50,000
equipment, bonding, workman's comp.,				
errors and omissions				
Film Arts Foundation @ 5% of final budget			$25,000	$25,000
BUDGET TOTAL	$13,000	$38,914	$525,851	$577,737

* * * * * * * * * * * * * * * * * * * *

Notes to the budget:
    Ratio: 20:1 - The necessity for shooting a documentary at this ratio is essential because of two important factors, the first being the inavailablity of Kodak film in the Soviet Union. All projected materials must be brought with us at the outset. The second factor is the style of the film making which is going to be cinema-verite and necessitates our being able to film spontaneous events as they occur.

    Travel: (Pre-production) - Research and Development consultations with advisors.

PAGE 6

TOWARD THE FUTURE:BUDGET

Income/Projections

INCOME:	ACTUAL		PROJECTED
	Cash	In kind	
Case Western Reserve University			
Foundations			$115,000
Organizations			$250,000
Sovenfilm, Moscow			$30,000
(portion of travel and related services)			
Miscellaneous Corporations/Businesses			$120,000
Diner-Allied Film Company		$7,674	
SRO		$5,000	
Gassers		$2,000	
Individuals			
Vergilia	$10,000		
Steven		$10,000	
Nelson S		$2,800	
Mary W		$3,000	
Natalie	$3,000		
Miscellaneous Individuals:			$16,000
TOTALS:	$13,000	$30,474	$531,000

BUDGET TOTAL $574,474

"At The River I Stand"

Project Description

Although usually remembered as the struggle which culminated in the assassination of Martin Luther King, Jr., the 1968 Memphis sanitation strike is significant in itself as a watershed event in the civil rights movement. As one of the last great dramas of that movement, the sixty-five day strike challenged the effectiveness of Dr. King's nonviolent philosophy in the increasingly violent decade of the 1960's. Moreover, it became the testing ground for the new and controversial direction being taken by his Poor People's Campaign, which merged civil rights issues with broader economic concerns. Indeed, his decision to become personally involved in the Memphis strike was based on his realization that the situation there was the concrete embodiment of this critical philosophical shift . Thus, as David Garrow notes in his Pulitzer-Prize winning biography of King, Bearing the Cross , King was convinced that` "the Memphis strike, with its clear portrayal of how issues of race and economics overlapped, and with the city's refusal to recognize its black workers and negotiate with them, was powerful evidence of just how important the Poor People's Campaign was for America's future."

Most print, film, and television histories that give accounts of the Memphis sanitation workers strike focus on it only as the event that resulted in King's assassination. Our documentary will be the first to render the specifics of the strike in great detail, and to examine it within a larger socio-historical context. The story of the Memphis sanitation strike is, on one level, a symbolically-charged story of opposing forces in American history: organized labor versus municipal authorities, civil disobedience versus civil law; poverty versus privilege, black versus white. On another level, it is a highly personal story of individual sacrifice and bravery, for the walkout of 1300 sanitation workers in February 1968 occurred not only without the sanction of the international union, but among people who, unlike thousands of black citizens throughout the Deep South, had no experience organizing and enduring the kind of resistance movement they were undertaking. It is also the story of failure: of how a national tragedy occurred in Memphis despite the arduous efforts of many people on both sides of the struggle to find a solution to the problem before violence erupted.

This documentary will be shaped by contextual questions: What was the history of the relationships between black workers and national unions, and between municipal governments and unions? Why did these men, so untrained and ill-prepared for long term protest action, and with so little initial encouragement from organized labor, take it upon themselves to strike? What were the lives of the workers and their families actually like before, during, and after the strike? Why at this time, so late in the nonviolent civil rights movement? Why in this particular city? And what can we learn from this tragic confluence of local events and national history?

The ninety-minute documentary will be composed of archival film footage and contemporary interviews shot on Betacam and will be completed on 1" video tape. Although our work will be informed by the guidance of a strong group of scholars, we hope to interview on camera only those who directly participated in the historical events that we will chronicle. As the highly acclaimed multi-part documentary of the civil rights movement, Eyes on The Prize, has made so dramatically clear, it is interviews with direct participants in historical events that make those events vivid, personal, and memorable. We will interview not only the most visible participants in this story--city council members, appointed officials, national civil rights and union leaders--but the rank and file strikers and their families as well. The success of Ken Burns' multi-part documentary on The Civil War has proven that history can be told from "the bottom - up," and not exclusively from "the top - down." This is especially true for our account of the Memphis sanitation strike, which began as a grassroots movement.

In 1968, immediately following the assassination of Dr. King, a bi-racial group of Memphis citizens formed a volunteer, non-profit community research and study group. Calling themselves the Memphis Search for Meaning Committee, the group undertook the monumental task of collecting as much material and information as they could in order to understand the events that had culminated in this tragedy. Years later, they were still at work, gathering documents, conducting audiotaped interviews, and applying for and receiving national grants for the indexing and preservation of what became known as the

Memphis Multi-Media Archival Project. These materials are now housed in the Mississippi Valley Collection in Memphis State University's Brister Library. The collection has drawn scholars from around the world intent on investigating the American civil rights movement. It is also an excellent archive of still photographs and over thirty hours of original film footage shot by local and national television cameras covering the strike. No less an authority than David Garrow refers to it as "undeniably the richest archive of local civil rights footage in existence." A great deal of the archival footage used in our project will come from this rich source. Other footage will be obtained from archives across the country.

Consultants

For this project we have assembled a group of consultants representing academia, labor, civil rights, and the local community. We have utilized, and will continue to utilize, our consultants in the following ways: to advise us on research methodologies; to critique our reading of historical events; to assess the accuracy and rigor with which we chronicle these events; and to inform us of alternative interpretations of (and perspectives on) the material available to us. More specific roles played by specific advisors follow below.

1. Dr. David Garrow, Professor of Political Science, City University of New York, New York, New York; Ph.D., Political Science, Duke University. As the recipient of the 1986 Pulitzer Prize for his book Bearing The Cross: Martin Luther King and the Southern Christian Leadership Conference, Dr. Garrow's expertise in the history of the civil rights movement has been invaluable to our project. Moreover, as a seasoned consultant on The Eyes on The Prize series, he has additional experience reviewing scripts and rough cuts, so we look forward to Dr. Garrow's continued participation.

2. Joan Turner Beifuss, M.A., English, Loyola University (Chicago). Currently an Instructor in the Memphis State English Department, she is the author of At The River I Stand, the definitive account of the sanitation strike. Moreover, her personal contacts with virtually every person we need to interview have already proven to be of immense practical value. The respect Ms. Beifuss commands among all who were involved in these events is enormous. Being associated with her has given us an immediate access that might otherwise not have come so easily.

3. Dr. Ken Goings, Professor, Department of History, Florida Atlantic University; Ph.D., History, Princeton University. Dr. Goings has published widely in the history of various aspects of the civil rights movement and has a strong scholarly interest in the images of African-Americans in popular culture.

4. Paul Stekler, Ph.D., Political Science, Harvard University. Dr. Stekler brings a dual perspective to our project. As a former assistant professor of Political Science at Tulane, he understands the importance of academic rigor and the complex qustions of methodology. In his more recent career as a historical documentary filmmaker, he co-produced two episodes of Eyes On The Prize, Part II, including the episode that devoted fifteen minutes to the Memphis strike. His experience in historical documentary filmmaking and his intimate knowledge of the material we are working with make him an ideal consultant.

5. David Yellin, Professor Emeritus, Department of Theatre & Communication Arts, Memphis State University. M.A., Columbia University. Mr. Yellin is the author of a classic text on television documentary and has taught documentary studies for two decades. As such, his critical perspective will be most useful in the development of our script. Even more important, however, is the fact that he headed the Memphis Search for Meaning Committee, and conducted many of the audio interviews with the key players in the events of 1968 that are now housed at the Mississippi Valley Collection.

6.Charles Crawford, Professor, Department of History, Memphis State University. Ph.D., History, Univ. of Mississippi. Dr. Crawford is widely respected as a specialist in the history of Tennessee and the mid-South region in particular. We call on his expertise in this area to give us a broader historical understanding of Memphis, and on his expertise in the methodology of oral history, a critical project area for which he serves as a guide and critical eye - ear.

7. David Lee Acey, Assistant Professor, Department of Theatre & Communication Arts, Memphis State University. M.A., Communication, Memphis State University. Professor Acey teaches Black Studies and was a participant in both Martin Luther King Memphis marches in l968. He will be interviewed as a participant, and consulted as a field research resource to supply script criticism from a Black Studies perspective.

8. Rev. James L. Netters, Rev. Netters played a key role in the events of l968. He has been interviewed about this role, and has provided introductions to other members of the black community with insightful and vivid memories of the sanitation strike.

9. Fred Ashwill, President, Memphis chapter, AFL-CIO; Business Manager, IBEW local 1288. Mr. Ashwill provides us with a valuable perspective on the history of labor in Memphis and is helping us gain access to labor archive materials.

10. Rev. S.B Kyles, Rev. Kyles was a major participant in these events and was with Dr. King at the time of his assassination. Still an important figure in the national civil rights movement, Rev. Kyles provides perspective on both the strike and its relationship to the national civil rights movement.

11. Rev. Frank McRae, Rev. McRae was also a major participant in these events and brings the insight not only of a direct participant, but of a pastor of a white, middle-class Methodist church. As such, he is able to discuss the response his parishioners had to the sanitation strike.

12. Carol Lynn Yellin, Ms. Yellin, a retired Reader's Digest editor, was equally responsible with her husband for spearheading the work of the Memphis Search for Meaning Committee, and it is from this perspective that we seek her advice.

Production History

In preparation for filming, the three co-producers have read extensively. Some volumes include Dr. Garrow's Bearing The Cross and his Martin Luther King and The F.B.I.; Taylor Branch's Parting The Waters: America in The Civil Rights Years; Joseph Goulden 's biography of Jerry Wurf, Jerry Wurf: Labor's Last Angry Man; Aldon Morris's The Origins of the Civil Rights Movement; Eric Foner's multi-volumed history of organized labor in the U.S.; and, of course, Joan Beifuss's At the River I Stand. We have also exhaustively researched the newspaper, magazine and photographic materials available to us at the Mississippi Valley Collection and at the Memphis Room of the Memphis-Shelby County Library. We have viewed all available motion picture footage on the strike, and have begun research at film archives in New York and Washington for material that will be necessary to purchase in order to place the Memphis events within a national context.

After writing an initial draft of the treatment, we submitted it with a grant application to The Southern Humanities Media Fund. (This application, for $46,432, was approved by SHMF in June.) Following this, we began shooting Interviews. (As of November, 1991 we have conducted 17 in-depth interviews, totalling over 1,500 minutes.)

Later in the summer, we convened a consultants' meeting to review our treatment. Their suggestions have been incorporated into our new draft.

Production Plan

During the Fall of 1991we have been busy transcribing interviews and raising funds. We plan to resume shooting interviews in December. By next August we will have shot all interviews and non-motion picture archival visual materials (newspapers, still photographs); gathered footage from national archives and negotiated rights with these archives and with music publishers; written a precise editing script; transfered all footage to videotape and made VHS window dubs for off-line editing; performed the off-line edit; convened our consultants to review the off-line edit; incorporated suggestions into the off-line fine cut (including the possible shooting of additional material); and commenced sound editing and sound effects work. The final off-line fine cut will then be taken to MPL Postmasters in Memphis for on-line video editing, including all graphic and any visual effects work that may be needed, and to APC (Audio Production Center) in Atlanta for audio re-recording and mixing; VHS dubs will be made from the master one inch tape for use in distribution negotiations and publicity.

Distribution Plan

Our primary intended audience is a national adult general public. The program will have additional life in university and high school classes dealing with the civil rights movement, Martin Luther King, the labor movement in the South, and the history of Memphis and the region.

No matter how well made, a film is not successful if it does not reach its audience. Accordingly, we consider the marketing and promotion of this film to be a vital part of its creation. Co-producer Steve Ross is experienced in this field, having negotiated contracts for his previous work with PBS, the Arts and Entertainment Network, and Pyramid Films. We will draw on this distribution and marketing expertise to help insure that At The River I Stand is seen by the widest audience possible.

Our plan is to find the best PBS venue for a national prime time television premiere, most likely on or near April 4, l993, the twenty-fifth anniversary of the strike and the assassination of Dr. King. As the attached letter from PBS programming executive Sandra Heberer indicates, the timing of this project could not have been more ideal from a programming perspective. (She has requested that we send her an off-line rough cut in July of 1992.)

We have received money from The Southern Humanities Media Fund to travel with the film for several screenings throughout Tennessee and neighboring states. The same fund has also granted us $600 for in-house computer design and laser-writer production of a simple, folded one-sheet brochure and for the reproduction of still photographs to be used for publicity purposes. Moreover, we will work with our consultants and supervise the production of a study guide/bibiliography that will accompany the film. Through Memphis State University printing services we will produce 1,000 copies of an attractively printed guide.   Co-producers Ross and Appleby are experienced in this area, having supervised the creation of study guides for their films The Invisible River and The Old Forest.

Project Personnel

 At The River I Stand is being written and produced by David Appleby, Dr. Allison Graham, and Steven John Ross. All three are Associate Professors in The Department of Theatre and Communication Arts at Memphis State University.

Professor Appleby, whose Master of Fine Arts Degree was earned at Temple University, is an award-winning documentary filmmaker and camera person whose work includes a film on the history of Memphis. He is chief videographer for this project.

Dr. Graham's Ph. D. is from The University of Florida. She is well known for her book on film maker Lindsay Anderson, for her essays on Film and American Culture, and as associate editor of Film Criticism. She has served as the co-director of the Women's Studies program at Memphis State.

Professor Ross received his Master's Degree from New York University in Cinema Studies. His award-winning documentary and fiction films have been shown at over a dozen national and international film festivals, and have been televised nationwide in prime time on PBS and The Arts and Entertainment Network.

Complete resumes for all three are available on request.

Applicant Organization

This film is a production of Memphis State University, a non-profit, tax-exempt, state-supported institution of higher education. Enrollment totals 15,146 students; 47.3 % men and 52.7% women. Doctoral degrees are offered in fourteen subject areas. During the fiscal year 1990-91 the university's office of sponsored programs received and successfully administered $10,578,643 in externally sponsored funds. Over the past decade the university has administered the production of several film projects by Ross and Appleby that have received funding from external sources.

Revised Budget (October 15, 1991) - 1968 Memphis Sanitation Strike Project
Project Period: July 1, 1991 - June 30, 1993

				Cost Sharing		
		SHMF	THC	(1)SHMF MSU	(2)THC MSU	Additional Funds
I.	Salaries and Wages					
	A. Project Director, Co-producer					
	Steve Ross					
	1. Summer 7/1/91-8/20/91					
	1 2/3 mos. @ 100%	3,000				
	2. Acad. year 8/21/91-12/31/91					
	4 1/3 mos @ 33%			6,099		
	3. Acad. yr. 1/1/92-5/20/92					
	4 2/3 mos. @ 43%		1,993	6,577		
	4. Summer 5/21/92-8/20/92					
	3 mos. @ 32%		2,049			2,049
	5. Acad. yr 8/22/92-12/21/92					
	4 mos. @ 33%			5,634		
	6. Acad. yr. 1/1/93-5/20/93					
	4 2/3 mos. @ 10%				1,993	
	B. Co-director, Co-producer					
	David Appleby					
	1. Summer 7/1/91-8/20/91					
	1 2/3 mos. @ 100%	3,000				
	2. Acad. yr. 8/21/91-5/20/92					
	9 mos. @ 33%			12,738		
	3. Summer 5/21/92-8/20/92					
	3 mos. @ 32%		2,059			2,059
	4. Acad. yr. 8/21/92-5/20/93					
	9 mos. @ 10%				3,860	
	C. Humanities Scholar, Co-producer					
	Allison Graham					
	1. Summer 7/1/91-8/20/91					
	1 2/3 Mos. @ 100%	3,000				
	2. Acad. yr. 8/21/91-5/20/92					
	9 mos. @ 33%			12,691		
	3. Summer 5/21/92-8/20/92					
	3 mos. @ 32%		2,051			2,051
	4. Acad. yr. 8/21/92-5/20/93					
	9 mos. @ 10%				3,846	
	D. Humanities Scholars					
	David Acey, Joan Beifuss, Bonnie Dill					
	1. Summer 7/1/91-8/20/91	450				
	E. Sound Recording/Camera Asst.					
	Thomas Dean					
	1. Summer 7/1/91-8/20/91					
	1 2/3 mos. @ 18%			537		
	SUBTOTAL 1	9,450	8,152	44,276	9,699	6,159

		SHMF	THC	(1)SHMF MSU	(2)THC MSU	Additional Funds
				Cost Sharing		
II.	Consultants					
	A. Narrator	1,600				
	B. Humanities Scholars	750				
	C. Assistant Editor	2,000				
	D. Assistant Camera					1,425
	E. Community Liaison					750
	SUBTOTAL II	4,350				2,175
III.	Fringe Benefits					
	A. 17.8% of IA1,A4,B1,B3,C1,C3,D1	1,682	1,096			1,096
	B. 24% of IA2,A3,A5,A6,B2,B4,C2,C4		478	8,919	2,328	
	C. 21% of E1			113		
	SUBTOTAL III	1,682	1,574	9,032	2,328	1,096
IV.	Production					
	A. Film, Video, Tape, Supplies	2,400				
	B. Sound Tape and Supplies	100				
	C. Editing Supplies & Services	6,200	3,000			
	D. Post Production Sound	5,800	3,000			3,200
	E. Usage Rights and Fees	11,000	4,000			38,000
	F. Lab Processing-Printing		10,000			16,000
	G. Study Guides, other material	600				
	H. Travel for Narrator and Consultants	2,200				2,000
	I. Transcriber		600			
	J. Production Vehicle Rental					1,000
	K. Local Travel (mileage)					700
	L. Betacam Rental					4,500
	SUBTOTAL IV	28,300	20,600			65,400
V.	Post Production					
	A. Humanities Evaluator		125			
	SUBTOTAL V		125			
VI.	Distribution					
	A. Duplicates/Prints/(2-1",10 VHS)	200		(450)		600
	B. Public Screening (6)	1,500				
	C. Brochures/Posters	500				
	D. Study Guide Distribution	150				
	SUBTOTAL VI	2,350		**(450)		600

		SHMF	THC	Cost Sharing (1)SHMF MSU	(2)THC MSU	Additional Funds
VII.	Project Administration					
	A. Postage and Telephone	300				500
	SUBTOTAL VII	300				500
	TOTAL DIRECT COSTS	46,432	30,451	53,308	12,027	75,930
VIII.	Indirect Costs					
	(Note-Since the University's established indirect cost rate under OMB A-88 is 51.3% of MTDC, the costs calculated at this rate may be considered a University contribution.)			51,116	21,791	
	TOTAL COSTS	46,432	30,451	104,424	33,818	75,930
	Funds requested THC	30,451				
	Funds awarded SHMF	46,432				
	University Cost Sharing	138,242				
	University In-Kind	450				
	Additional costs to be raised	75,930				
	Total Project Costs	291,505				

SHMF = Southern Humanities Media Fund
THC = Tennessee Humanities Council

**In-Kind MSU Contribution

Summary of Budget and Funding Sources

Organization Memphis State University

Project "At The River I Stand": 90 min. Documentary

Total Project Budget $ 291,505

Project Funding Sources:

Organization	Amount Requested	Amount Received
J Roderick MacArthur Foundation	$ 20,000	$ Pending
Memphis State U. Cost Share Contribution	$138,242	$138,242
Memphis State U. In Kind Contribution	450	450
Southern Humanities Media Fund	46,432	46,432
Tennessee Humanities Council	30,451	Pending
Michael Moore	15,000	Pending
The Levinson Foundation	10,000	Pending
The A T & T Foundation	10,000	Pending
The Rockefeller Foundation	30,000	Pending
The Ford Foundation	30,000	Pending
The Lilly Endowment	20,000	Pending
Totals	**$ 350,575**	**$ 185,124**

Memphis State
U N I V E R S 19 November 1991

(901) 678-2565

Program Office
Lilly Endowment Inc.
Post Office Box 88068
Indianapolis, IN 46208

To The Lilly Endowment:

I am one of three producers of a documentary film project that we think the Lilly Endowment will be interested in supporting.

Our project, tentatively titled <u>At the River I Stand</u>, is about the 1968 Memphis sanitation workers' strike. It will explore how an event that seemed of interest only to one Southern city became of national and international significance when it led to the assassination of Dr. Martin Luther King, Jr. This 90-minute documentary will be completed by September, 1992, in ample time for PBS airing in April, 1993, the twenty-fifth anniversary of the strike and of Dr. King's assassination. (Enclosed you'll find a letter of support from a PBS programming executive.)

Two of the Lilly Endowment's major concerns, urban ministry and the theme of religion and public life, are essential subjects of our documentary. Dr. King's expanding philosophy of the scope of Christian social responsibility led to his public support of the sanitation workers' strike. He saw in the struggling Memphis movement, in fact, the concrete embodiment of his newly born Poor People's Campaign, which merged civil rights issues with broader economic concerns. As biographer David Garrow has written in <u>Bearing The Cross,</u> King was convinced that "the Memphis strike, with its clear portrayal of how issues of race and economics overlapped, and with the city's refusal to recognize its black workers and negotiate with them, was powerful evidence of just how important the Poor People's Campaign was for America's future." It was the Memphis strike which became the final crucible of his egalitarian religious and moral commitments.

College of Communication and Fine Arts
Department of Theatre and Communication Arts/Memphis, Tennessee 38152

An Equal Opportunity/Affirmative Action University

Before Dr. King was an active participant in these events, however, African-American churches in Memphis had already become deeply involved in the strike and were affirming Dr. King's vision of the role of churches in social change. Their participation was reluctant at first, and deemed inappropriate by some, but as events progressed, the churches became the spiritual and practical home for the cause, and the ministers themselves became leaders of what quickly became a community movement.

The Rev. James Lawson, one of the major theoreticians of the national civil rights strategy of nonviolence, emerged as the key spokesman and tactician for this coalition of sanitation workers and the church. As he had done in Nashville seven years earlier, Rev. Lawson adapted the practice of peaceful protest to the exigencies of a major Southern city in crisis, training and inspiring a community of workers for a prolonged struggle. (It was at Rev. Lawson's request, moreover, that his old friend Martin King would come to Memphis.)

White Memphis clergy also became embroiled in the strike. Some were torn between personal conscience and the wishes of their parishioners, the great majority of whom saw the strike an an unwelcomed threat to the status quo. Others, like some of their African-American counterparts, tempered their sympathy for the workers with a distrust of the motives of the international union. Attempts were made by an interdenominational group of clergy to bridge the racial gap between themselves and their African-American colleagues, and some attempted to persuade Memphis power brokers that the strike had become much larger than just another municipal labor issue. Although these clergy tried to act as mediators throughout the two-month crisis, the city government's refusal to negotiate with the union led to mounting racial tensions, violence, and, eventually, the assassination of Dr. King.

Often overlooked in this story, however, is the settlement of the strike less than two weeks after the assassination. The official recognition of the most socially and economically vulnerable workers in the city was a victory hardly anyone in the labor or civil rights movements could have predicted. It was a victory made possible by the unity and support of the black churches, and by their clergy's unwavering commitment, despite considerable pressure from those impatient with the system, to the principles of peaceful social change. What religious scholar Cornel West has said of Dr. King is equally true of these leaders, for their dream, like his, was "grounded and refined in the black church experience, supplemented by liberal Christianity, implemented by Gandhian methods of nonviolent resistance, and rooted in American ideals." And although the tragedy of Dr. King's assassination often dominates accounts of the Memphis strike, it is the success--not the failure--of this dream to mobilize and sustain an entire community that we believe is at the heart of the story.

We have assembled a distinguished list of advisors and consultants for <u>At the River I Stand</u>, including Pulitzer Prize-winning King biographer Dr. David Garrow, and Dr. Paul Stekler, producer of two episodes of the civil rights documentary series <u>Eyes on The Prize</u>. Several clergy who played crucial roles in the events we will chronicle are serving as consultants and/or have agreed to be interviewed on camera for the film. These include leading national religious and civil rights leaders Rev. Andrew

Young, Rev. Benjamin Hooks, Rev. Joseph Lowery, Rev. Billy Kyles, Rev. James Orange, and Rev. Lawson, as well as Memphis religious and civic leaders Rev. Frank MacRae and Rev. James Netters.

We have been working on this project for almost two years, and have received support ($46,000) from the Southern Humanities Media Fund. We also have a grant application pending for $30,000 at the Tennessee Humanities Council. The proposal has received very strong support at the September board meeting of the Council. Their only area of concern, however, was that we find the $75,000 of additional funding needed to complete the project. We are currently seeking parts of this funding from several sources.

We are experienced filmmakers with several awards and national broadcasts on PBS and the Arts and Entertainment Network to our credit. Upon request I will send you a VHS tape containing excerpts from three of our previous films: The Old Forest, an adaptation of Peter Taylor's story; The Invisible River, a documentary on the historical relationship between Memphis and the Mississippi; and Searching For Wordin Avenue, a documentary about a turn-of-the-century Hungarian immigrant community.

We have completed over forty hours of broadcast-quality interviews for this project and a 23-page treatment that describes in detail our vision of the finished film. If you think our project is of sufficient interest to The Lilly Enowment, I will send you a complete proposal, resumes, a comprehensive budget, the treatment, and the video cassette sample of our previous work.

Sincerely,

Steven John Ross,
Co-Producer
Associate Professor

L I L L Y
ENDOWMENT
+ I N C +

A private,
family
foundation
since 1937

February 19, 1992

Stephen John Ross
Co-Producer
Associate Professor
College of Communication and Fine Arts
Memphis State University
3745 Central Avenue
Memphis, Tennessee 38125

Dear Dr. Ross:

Thank you for the information on your film project "At The River I Stand." I regret to report that funds for projects in the media (publications, television, films, theater) are no longer available. Our Board of Directors has determined that other areas of the Endowment's interests ought to take higher priority during this period of scarce resources.

Your efforts to document the overlap of race and economics as concretized in the Memphis strike is important and certainly deserves support. Best wishes in your search for other sources of funding.

Sincerely,

Jacqui Burton

Jacqui Burton
Program Director, Religion

JB:sdh

2801 North Meridian Street
Post Office Box 88068
Indianapolis, Indiana 46208
(317)924-5471 Fax: (317)926-4431

SOLICITING INDIVIDUAL DONORS: DO'S AND DON'TS

By Sally Jo Fifer

An Interview with Peter Adair, film and videomaker and partner of Adair and Armstrong, an independent video production company.

VN: Who are donors and which of your projects depended on donors?

PA: I am going to talk about donors versus investors. It is important to make that distinction because the pitch is different. If you are proposing that the film is a money-making proposition, which is a joke, it is a very different process. If the film is going to make money then that is an added incentive but no one in their right mind would invest in a political film to make money. *Holy Ghost People, Stopping History,* and *The AIDS Show* all involved donors.

VN: What percentage of the funding came from donors?

PA: The majority.

VN: I was surprised to read that 83% of all charitable contributions come from individuals. Of course, many of those dollars are in the form of religious donations - you don't have your own cable channel - how have you managed to be so successful at raising money from individuals?

PA: Because I am too stupid to stop. It has been nothing but persistence. Actually my first real experience began with getting investors for *Word is Out.* It was obvious that there was no other source of funding for the film. I determined I was going to make that film come hell or high water. The first thing I did was talk to foundation experts who knew a lot about raising money, not for film, but for other projects. The advice I got from all of them was to forget it. Back in '73 there was really no money for film. The subject matter was so forbidden I didn't even try foundation fundraising. At that point I wasn't aware of many other films that had been funded by individuals so I developed some principles of my own.

The first and perhaps most important principle is that you have to realize that you are selling your film. You have to figure out what is in it for the other person. No matter how noble you are or how much guilt you can use, if you haven't found out what is in it for them, I don't think you are going to be successful. And this principle applies across the board, from attracting investors to seeking funding from corporations or foundations.

VN: What is in it for a donor to give money to a film/video project?

PA: People will give money because they believe in the cause or the work, because it is prestigious, because they like you.

VN: What has been your most successful approach to donors?

PA: We have raised most of our money through fundraising parties. Ultimately, I found that it wasn't worth it to spend a lot of time with a few individuals with a lot of money. This is just my experience. In 1973 there weren't many, and now there are - but they are spreading their money around.

I started with my friends. I didn't know anyone rich. I made a list of everyone I knew and how they could help me - with advice, rich friends, etc. No matter who you know, you know someone of influence, or you know someone who knows someone of influence. It doesn't make sense to make up a list of fat cats whom you have never heard of and who have never heard of you.

Try and get the name of a person who wants to help and who has a house with production value. First ask them for money Then go to the second position which is to ask if they know people with money. Then go to the third position - if they are still open - and ask to hold a fundraiser at their house. It must be a lovely house with prestige. If you have a fundraiser at your flat in the Mission, the project is going to be taken less seriously. People know how expensive media is and you have to show them, not that you are rich, but that you have access to some money.

Ideally, you want your host to invite their friends. You want to mix their friends with people you know. You do all the work under the host's name It is extremely important that it looks like the invitation comes from the host. They may have stationary or you have some printed up. Then they can write little notes like "Dear Mary, I hope you can come. This is something I am excited about."

If the host is cooperative, then they will write these notes, but they should at least sign them. Then see if you can get the host to call the most important people a week ahead of time. They should make this fundraiser a social obligation. It is important to let them know there is going to be a fundraising pitch. They will agree to this if they believe in what you are doing, that it will be a good evening and if they feel that you aren't going to embarrass them.

You may want to fold in your own people - those whom you haven't wanted to talk to one to one. One to one is very difficult. People have trouble saying "no." They will say no to you in their heads, so you don't want to corner them. Invite them so that they can see what you are doing. You write all your invitations and call your contacts to make sure that they are going to come.

VN: Do people generally come to fundraisers?

PA: You have to expect that only a small percentage of people will come. A film/videomaker must never be depressed because people don't come to these. You simply have to do everything to ensure that they will come.

VN: When is the best time for a fundraising party?

PA: Friday is good from 6 p.m. to 7:30 p.m. - in time for people to go out to dinner.

VN: What happens at the fundraiser?

PA: Some hosts may not give you money but will supply wine and hors d'oeuvres. If they don't do it you should get wine and good cheeses. I've always shown something. With *Word is Out*, we showed initial interviews on black and white half-inch reels. It was really primitive, but the minute you saw it, you knew we were on to something. It is good if you can do a little bit of shooting. That is one reason I switched to videotape because you can shoot sooner without spending a lot of money if you can hustle the equipment. With film it can cost you a fortune by the time you open the first can. Ultimately, video may not be cheaper than film but the start-up curve is much slower.

I try to make the reel as emotional and provocative as possible. We put a lot of energy into the reel. The reel can take us a month because it has to work on its own and move fast. That is very difficult. I sort of enjoy doing it because it makes you think a lot about the project.

It is extremely important to keep the sample reel short. If you show ten minutes and it is good then your audience is going to imagine that the rest of your project is that good. If you show a long piece with lots of problems then people are going to mistake it for the real one. They will imagine your final piece with the same deficiencies. It is very hard for people to understand the difference between a rough cut and the final product.

VN: Do you need to give people a press packet or donation envelope?

PA: Yes, it is important to pass out something for people to see. It doesn't have to be long, the nicer the better, but you don't want to make it look like you are wasting money. People like to take something home. You should explain what you are doing, what the budget is, perhaps what $100 will buy, what $1,000 will buy. The trick is to start with a high figure so that people won't give you $50 if they see a box marked for $75.

The figure should be a little higher figure than what you think the bottom amount will be. This can also backfire because the $1,000 people check the box for $100 and get off the hook. If you have guts you can use the negative option plan like the record mail order companies; you get the record if you don't send the card back. You keep a guest list through cards which everyone fills out. This is extremely important and where the real work begins; you go home and figure out who they are, where they came from, who invited them, and so on. On the cards that you collect as they leave you should have a box that saying, "I would like to help. Please give me a call," as well as a box that says, "Don't call me." Essentially, if they don't check the "Don't call me" box, they have given you permission to call them. This is important. You want to feel comfortable calling them.

It is highly unlikely that you will get checks in the mail or at the fundraiser unless you were terrific at giving the pitch. The next day and no later than two days afterwards you must do the calls. The longer you wait the quicker even the most enthusiastic will cool down no matter how high their enthusiasm was during the screening.

VN: What do you say when you call them?

PA: Ask them if they had any feedback on the tape and then say, "I hope we can expect a check." Those who are friendly, you can probably get to give parties and then the whole thing sort of springboards.

VN: You don't want to pass the hat at the fundraiser?

PA: You don't want to give people an excuse to give only a few bucks. You can do fundraising where you want more people to come and you pass the hat but I'm talking about the kind of fundraising where you are dealing with people who you want to make a donation of $500 to $1,000.

All of your success is dependent on how good the pitch is. It should be very brief, very direct, and very aggressive, but not so aggressive that the host is embarrassed. You usually do not want the host doing it and the host will often want to do it because they don't want to have to be embarrassed by you hitting too hard. You have to play that one very carefully. This is where the success comes if you are very good. Often it is best if you don't do it, especially if you know someone terrific or if you have a producer who is good at it. Then you can play the artist who doesn't touch filthy lucre and can walk around the party chatting.

VN: How long is the lead time?

PA: It takes about six weeks. By the time you talk to the host, print the invitations, and send them out, you have to plan that much ahead.

VN: It really works?

PA: The nice thing about this manner of fundraising is that if you have the patience and the charm and you have a project that is worthwhile on a subject which someone can believe it, it always works - unlike foundations or CPB where you don't know what they are going to do. Though it can be arduous, it is the most effective method.

The danger of soliciting individuals is that you can spend months massaging some ego and then you'll end up with 100 bucks; it is much more straight-forward to have this fancy party to find donors who are really interested in giving you money.

VN: Any last words of wisdom?

PA: Never leave anything up to the donors; it will never happen. People look for a reason not to give you money. To actually part with money is very difficult. Even though you spend it in your head, actually writing out the check is hard. Never leave it to your donor no matter how good hearted they are. Half of one percent of the time I ever showed a sample reel at a fundraiser did a fat check arrive in the mail two days later; you always have to call them.

Sometimes you have to call them five and six times. The only thing to be careful about is to stop at the point where you are annoying them. However, that is much farther than anyone would guess. Essentially, people like attention.

This article first appeared in *Video Networks*, the monthly newsletter of Bay Area Video Coalition, and is reprinted with their kind permission.

𝒱ideo 𝓗ouse 𝒫arty
Index

"The Video House Party" guide is reprinted
with the kind permission of: THE VIDEO PROJECT:
FILMS FOR A SAFE AND SUSTAINABLE WORLD,
5332 College Ave., Suite 101, Oakland, CA 94618.
(510) 655-9050 Fax (510) 655-9115.

THE VIDEO PROJECT

is the nation's leading non-profit distributor
of documentaries on critical global issues, including
Oscar Winners **Women - For America, For the World,
Deadly Deception** and **The Panama Deception**
and Emmy Winner **Dark Circle**.

Tax-Deductible Donations

help The Video Project reach millions of people by promoting
our programs to thousands of colleges, schools, libraries,
churches, community groups and concerned individuals.
Our current catalog offers approximately 200 compelling programs
on the challenges of the 1990's:
preserving the environment, seeking alternatives to war,
and creating a more liveable, just world.
These are award-winning programs which you will rarely see on T.V.

Our Goal

is to raise $100,000 from donors this year
to implement the following projects:

- Our nationwide **"Teaching the Next Generation" Campaign**
  will help educate and inspire hundreds of thousands of young people
  to care for our fragile planet. In January of 1993, we mailed our
  Eco-Video Collection for Schools Catalog to nearly 50,000
  K-12 schools, providing them with access to 45 highly rated
  environmental videos on issues including recycling, rainforests and
  endangered species. The response was tremendous, with orders
  coming in from every state. This September, with help from
  contributors, we anticipate reaching all 125,000 schools, plus a
  good number of district media centers and libraries, with an updated
  Eco-Video Catalog.

- The donation of Eco-Videos to economically disadvantaged and
  ethnically diverse schools.

- The promotion of thematic collections of videos on issues such as:
  **"Economics, the Environment and Sustainable
  Development," "Alternative Energy and Transportation,"**
  and **"The Global Fight for Ancient Forests."**

**Thank you for your offer to host a Video
House Party. Your party is a major contribution to
The Video Project, bringing in new financial support
and spreading the word about the work we do.
Equally important, you are helping to activate the
uninvolved and re-inspire the discouraged.**

Message from The Video Project President and Co-Founder Vivienne Verdon-Roe:

I had to raise $40,000 to produce **Women - For America, For the World**. I had applied to 50 foundations for grants to make the film. All of them turned me down, except one. Usually an optimistic soul, I felt positively depressed! However, I had good friends who believed in my work. I called ten of them and asked them to host a party in their home to help raise funds for my film's production.

There were surprises. The biggest one was this: these parties were fun! They were more than just fundraisers. They were empowering for all of us. We don't often have an opportunity to voice our concerns. When people get together and see others care, we feel supported in our concern. The open acknowledgement was reinforcing. And we were ready to go on to the next step - Action.

It was very gratifying to drive home after one of the parties with a pocket full of checks and offers to hold more parties. It was equally as rewarding to see that the occasion was a turning point for some of the guests.

In two years, we held over a hundred parties. Over 2,000 people attended, and the $40,000 was raised! In 1987, **Women - For America, For the World** went on to win an **Oscar**!!

Thank you so much for giving of your time and energy to further our work to create a safer, saner world. Together we <u>do</u> make a difference.

166

Responsibilities for Hosting
a Video House Party Fundraiser

1. **Recruit co-hosts; choose date, time, location.** You will probably enjoy the experience of planning, preparing and holding the party much more if you work with a couple of other people. Call friends and recruit co-hosts. (By co-hosting, it will be easier to come up with a large guest list, and you can also share expenses.) Decide who has the most suitable home for the party. The Video Project will provide a selection of video clips, comprising an approximately 30 minute program. If you feel you would prefer to show a specific half-hour video, please feel free to discuss it with us.

2. **Prepare mailing list and send out invitations.** Our goal is a minimum of 20-25 guests at each party. In order to get that turn-out, you will need to send out 80-100 invitations. Invite friends, neighbors, relatives, co-workers, and members of your church or synagogue and political groups. The Video Project will provide invitations and envelopes. One side of the invitation will be pre-printed, and on the other side, we will laser print your personal invitation to guests (see attached sample). Your contribution will include the postage.

3. **Telephone calls.** 14 days prior to the party, make calls to those who have not yet RSVP'd. <u>This is very important!</u> As people receive a lot of mail, they must be *personally* reminded and encouraged to attend. If a guest cannot attend, let them know more about the goals of The Video Project and suggest they send a contribution. A few days before the event, if you have the time, it is also helpful to telephone everyone who has RSVP'd as a further reminder.

4. **Provide Color TV and VCR.** The color TV monitor needs to be a minimum of 19 inches in order for guests to be able to see the picture well. The VCR must be a VHS machine (rather than a Sony Betamax or 8mm). *(See page 9 for TV & VCR Checklist.)*

5. **Prepare refreshments.** They can be as simple or elaborate as you choose. For instance, wine, cheese & fruit, or coffee, tea & cookies. The Video Project does have some mineral water, coffee, decaf, tea, sugar, paper cups and napkins. For those who need help in providing refreshments, we can contribute these items for as long as they last.

TIMELINE AND CHECKLIST
FOR HOSTING A VIDEO HOUSE PARTY FUNDRAISER

(see sample Dateline on next page)

☐ **30 days before the event** Recruit friends to co-host with you. Meet with them to set a date, time and place. Make a guest list, assign tasks. Discuss program choice.

☐ **21 days** Send out 80-100 invitations. Check with co-hosts to see that their invitations have been sent.

☐ **16 - 12 days** Call guest list for RSVP. Make sure co-hosts have called their guest lists, too.

☐ **10 days** When all the guests have been contacted once, check with co-hosts to see that at least 30 guests have confirmed. (Confirmed means "yes" not "maybe".) If you have 30 confirmations, you can assume 20 guests will attend.

☐ **4 days** Time permitting, all co-hosts begin reconfirmation calls to RSVP list.

☐ **2 days** Complete reconfirmation calls.

☐ **the day of the event** Ask your co-hosts to join you at least one hour before the party to set up, prepare refreshments, etc. Make sure the arrangements for the TV and VCR are settled previously.

☐ **1 day after the event** Call people who did not show up. Find out what happened, describe what they missed, and ask them for a contribution.

☐ **2 days after the event** The Video Project will send thank you notes to everyone who made a contribution, although you may choose to send more personalized ones.

Video House Party Dateline
(*Sample*)

Recruit Co-Hosts and Plan	Wednesday, January 1, 1992
Send Invitations	Friday, January 10, 1992
RSVP Calls	Friday, January 17, 1992
Confirmation Calls	Tuesday, January 21, 1992
Reconfirmation Calls	Monday, January 27, 1992
Complete Reconfirmation Calls	Wednesday, January 29, 1992
VIDEO HOUSE PARTY	**Friday, January 31, 1992**
No-Show Calls	Saturday, February 1, 1992
Send Thank You Notes (optional)	Sunday, February 2, 1992

The Evening's Program

1. As guests arrive, they will be asked to sign The Video Project guest book and will be given name tags to put on. Catalogs will be available and videotapes will be on display and for sale. Those who sign up as members will receive a free video from a selected group.

2. Serve refreshments as your guests arrive.

3. Begin the program by explaining why you are hosting the event and thank your guests for coming. Introduce The Video Project representative who will conduct the program. She will make a few introductory remarks and then ask the guests to introduce themselves and briefly state their reasons for attending the event.

4. She will then give some background information about The Video Project and briefly introduce the video clips, an approximately 35 minute program, (or a 30 minute video, if you have chosen to concentrate on one videotape of particular interest to your guests).

5. Following the video program, the Video Project representative will give more information about the organization and its goals and ask people to make contributions, become members, and/or help to organize more Video House Parties.

6. Guests will then be given some quiet time to consider their donation. Hand out donation cards and envelopes. (As The Video Project is a non-profit organization, donations are tax deductible to the extent the law permits.)

7. The Video Project representative will then pass around donation collection baskets and open the floor for a discussion of responses to the video clips, questions about The Video Project, general and specific concerns for the planet and about how to get involved, etc.

8. At the close of the group discussion, she will then thank the guests and co-hosts for making the party possible/successful.

9. Guests will then have time to browse through catalogs, pick up a membership packet and free video if they've become a member, buy videos, and enjoy refreshments.

10. Co-hosts stay to clean up and celebrate!

Sample Timeline of Evening's Program

(If Party is 7:30 pm - 10:00 pm)

6:00-7:30   Hosts prepare refreshments, TV/VCR set-up, etc.

7:30   Guests arrive, sign-in, put on name tags, and may look at catalog and videotapes. Time for socializing and refreshments.

8:00   Hosts gather guests together, make introductory remarks and introduce The Video Project representative.

8:05   The Video Project representative makes introductory remarks and welcomes the guests, asking them to briefly state why they came to the party. She thanks them and introduces the video program.

8:20   She shows video clips of current work (about 35 minutes), or, alternatively, just one half-hour documentary is shown.

8:55   The Video Project representative will give more information about the organization and its goals and ask people to make contributions, become members, and/or help to organize more Video House Parties. Donation envelopes are handed out. Quiet time for considerating donations. Donations collected. More discussion and questions fielded.

9:15   Party continues with more refreshments, socializing and discussions. Videotapes can be bought, free tapes given to new members, etc.

10:00   Party over. Clean-up and Celebrate!

Familiar Pitfalls in Hosting
a Video House Party Fundraiser

1. **Doing it all yourself.** For many, it is easier to do something alone rather than to seek help. However, you might find it a strain to do all the inviting and preparations that make a really successful event. In contrast, two or three people working together will find that hosting an event is very manageable and more fun.

2. **Delaying or avoiding phoning your guests**. There are a million distractions from making your calls, but to have a successful event, you must make phone calls. People get a lot of mail. They must be *personally* encouraged to attend. If a group of you can phone together from a place with enough phones, you will have a better time.

3. **Prejudging who will be interested in attending.** Repeatedly, people tell us how surprised they were that so-and-so was interested enough to attend and contribute.

4. **Assuming your guests will show up.** You have invited people to attend an event where they will hear and talk about some difficult issues, such as environmental problems and war. Additionally, they will be asked to give money: double jeopardy! People will attend out of their overriding concern for a safe and secure world, but it will probably take your encouragement - that's what brings out their concern.

    You can do this by extending yourself - let your friends know why this is important to you, ask questions, and listen to whatever concerns your friends may have. Remember to communicate the focus of the event - **hope** - and what each of us can do to make a difference.

TV & VCR CHECKLIST

☐ At least a 19" color TV

☐ A VHS videocassette player

☐ Any necessary extension cords

☐ Cables and proper adaptors for attaching VCR and TV

*It is a good policy to set up the TV and VCR
to make sure everything is working
well before the last minute!!*

How to Use a Videocassette Recorder (VCR)

1. VCR's are very easy to use. Have someone who knows how to use a VCR show you if you don't already know how. (If need be, you can generally rent a VCR from your local video store for $10.)

2. Most half-inch videocassettes are now VHS. Make sure that your VCR is for use with VHS tapes (not BETA). We will bring the VHS tape.

3. The VCR and TV both need to be plugged into an electrical socket. The cable from the VCR needs to be connected to the TV. You might need a TV "adaptor" for older TV's (available at TV stores or with a rental VCR).

4. Turn the TV to channel 3 or 4, depending on which has a blank channel space. Alternatively, some TV's have a TV/VCR switch.

5. Turn on the VCR. Press "play."

6. If the image on the screen has white flashes through it, adjust the small "tracking" wheel/knob on the front section of your recorder. Turn the wheel/knob in either direction until the image is perfect.

7. Check your sound so that all your audience can hear.

8. If there is a large audience, set the TV up high enough for all to see.

Please Join us For
A Special Showing of the
Academy Award -
winning film:

Women —
For America,
For The World

A Fundraiser For:

Renew your Hope! This film has touched the hearts of millions. We will be using this opportunity to increase our commitment and to discuss specific ways we can contribute to a more peaceful and secure world.

Date:

Time:

Host:

Address:

Phone:

SAMPLE INVITATION

A FUND-RAISER FOR

_____

Your contribution will support

_____

_____

☐   I would like to contribute $ _____

Please make checks payable to: _____

Name: _____

Street Address: _____

City, State & Zip Code: _____

Telephone #: (_____) _____

☐   please contact me:

☐   I would like to give a wine & cheese party

☐   I would like to volunteer time to assist your work

DONATION CARD

Join *Maud's* Credit Roll:

Alternative Mortgage Sources
Astraea Foundation
Lesley Anderson MD
Cara Aron
"The Bettys"
Trilby Boone
Janet E. Brown
Linda J. Burnett
Julie M. Byrne
Chicago Resource Center
Barbara Deming Memorial
Editel
Brandy & Jenny Elger
Foundation for Creative Arts
Ginger Elliot
Empowerment Project
Lillian Faderman & Phyllis Irwin
Film Arts Foundation
The Film Bank
Frameline Inc.
Pan Haskins & Esther Orioli
Page Hodel
Horizons Foundation
Kathleen Hurley
Susan Johnson & Constance Wolfe
Yvonne D. King & Joni Anderson
Al & Carol Kiss
Rebecca Logrbrinck
Dr. Debra Morris & Dr. Anita Booth
Tanya Neiman
Michael Peredo
Marcia Perlstein & Nyla Gladden
Philanthrofund
Morgan R. Pinney Trust
Pioneer Fund
Rachel Pray & Laura Weinstock
Printz Electronic Design Services
Jane Rule & Helen Sonthoff
Val Scott
Alissa Shethar
Skylight Productions
Studio Miramar
Jean Swallow
Katherine Syromiatnikoff
Tassahara Bakery
Ann Telthorst
Louise I. Vargo (in memory)
Mary Warren
Elaine J. Womack
Cedric Yap

Dear Friend,

I'm the producer of *Last Call at Maud's*, a lively documentary that takes you to closing night at two landmark lesbian bars in San Francisco -- Maud's and Amelia's. Several superstars of the lesbian scene came to pay their respects as these famous places served their last drinks. Pioneers such as Sally Gearhart, Judy Grahn, Phyllis Lyon, Del Martin, JoAnn Loulan, Gwenn Craig, Pat Norman, Mary Wings, Nisa Donnelly, Jo Daly and Rikki Streicher have contributed priceless interviews and rare visuals to make this a fascinating look at where lesbian culture has been and where it's going.

Producing a documentary is never easy, but I am continually encouraged by the support our community offers. The high production values and quality of this film are due to the work of dozens of professionals who have generously donated their expertise and production facilities to ensure that this one-of-a-kind film reaches the widest possible audience.

Small grants and private donations have made it possible for us to bring this film near completion, but there's more that needs to be done.

As we wrap up production, <u>you</u> have the opportunity to play a major role in completing this groundbreaking film. With a contribution of $100, your name will be included in the *Last Call at Maud's* credit roll. For $200, you can immortalize your name and the name of someone you love, **plus** receive a first-edition copy of the *Last Call at Maud's* video cassette. By the way, contributions of any amount will speed up completion, and each will be recognized with a gift card.

Your generosity now, more than ever, is vitally important. So, show your star quality and help make movie magic. You'll not only be sharing the big screen with great company, you'll be giving a gift to yourself and your community that will outlast a lifetime.

Sincerely,

Paris Poirier
Producer/Director

Yes, I want to make film herstory!

☐ **$200** (two screen credits plus the videocassette)
☐ **$100** (one screen credit)
☐ **$20** (gift card)
☐ $_____

Method of Payment:
☐ Check
☐ Mastercard*
☐ VISA*

Please make checks payable to The Maud's Project.
☐ I want my contribution to be tax-deductible.

Donor:
Name _____
Address _____
_____
_____

MAKE MOVIE MAGIC!

Screen Credit #1:
Name _____
Address _____
_____

Screen Credit #2:
Name _____
Address _____
_____

*Credit Card Information
Account No. _____
Expiration Date _____ Phone _____
Signature _____

PLACE
STAMP
HERE

The Maud's Project

32A Horizon Avenue
Venice, California 90291

177

CONSULT WITH THE AUTHOR

Morrie Warshawski consults with individual clients or organizations either in-person or by phone. He can present a popular workshop, **How to Get Grants for Film and Video**, in half-day, full-day or two-day versions in your community.

Photo by Joe Angeles

Warshawski's specialties include: long-range planning, career guidance, fundraising training and strategies, critique of specific proposals, marketing and distribution. He works with clients on a one-time or on-going basis, subject to his availability.

Clients have included:

Dozens of individual film and video producers throughout the US

The National Endowment for the Arts/Media Arts
    and Advancement Programs
The Center for New Television
WGBH/Contemporary Artists' Television Fund
The Council on Foundations
The Bush Foundation
The MacArthur Foundation
The California Arts Council
The Missouri Arts Council
KDHX Radio and TV
The South Carolina Arts Commission

He is also interested in hearing comments and suggestions from readers of *Shaking the Money Tree*. For more information contact:

Morrie Warshawski
6364 Forsyth Blvd.
St. Louis, MO 63105

BOOKS FROM

MICHAEL WIESE PRODUCTIONS

FILM & VIDEO BUDGETS

by Michael Wiese

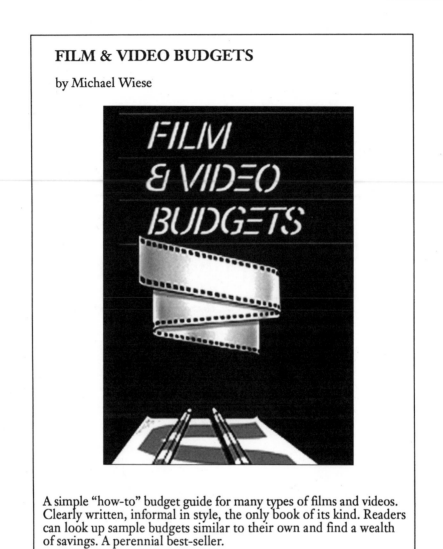

A simple "how-to" budget guide for many types of films and videos. Clearly written, informal in style, the only book of its kind. Readers can look up sample budgets similar to their own and find a wealth of savings. A perennial best-seller.

$18.95, 348 pp., 18 budgets, ISBN 0-941188-02-7

PRODUCER TO PRODUCER
The Best of Michael Wiese from VIDEOGRAPHY Magazine

by Michael Wiese

Edited by Brian McKernan,
Editor, VIDEOGRAPHY

Current information about producing, financing, marketing and creativity is vital to the videomaker. Michael Wiese's "Producer to Producer" column in *VIDEOGRAPHY* magazine has provided independent producers with cutting-edge insights on the business of video: program development, production, financing, marketing and distribution.

In an informal and entertaining style, Mr. Wiese draws on his own experience and that of other successful video producers to demonstrate forward-thinking industry practices.

Includes: "Shaking the Money Tree," "Zen and the Art of the Steadicam, Jr.," "Where Do you Get the Money?," "Infomercials: Where's the Info?," "Self-Distribution," "You Can Make Desktop Video–But Can You Sell It?" and much more.

176 pp., illustrations
$19.95, ISBN: 0-941188-15-9

FILM & VIDEO FINANCING

by Michael Wiese

Praised as a book that prepares producers to get the money! A "palette" of creative strategies for producers in financing their feature films and video projects. Interviews with the producers of "sex, lies & videotape," "Trip to Bountiful," and "T2."

$22.95, 300 pp., ISBN 0-941188-11-6

THE WRITER'S JOURNEY
Mythic Structure for Storytellers & Screenwriters

by Christopher Vogler

An insider's look at how master storytellers from Lucas to Spielberg have used mythic structure to create powerful stories which tap into the mythological core which exists in us all.

Writers will discover step-by-step guidelines and learn how to structure plots and create realistic characters. A Hollywood studio head made the rough draft for this book required reading for his entire executive staff.

$22.95, 283 pp.
ISBN 0-941188-13-2

FILM & VIDEO MARKETING
by Michael Wiese

Secrets of marketing you can use today! This insiders' book shares industry marketing techniques you can use with investors, exhibitors, audiences, distributors, home video suppliers, wholesalers and retailers. You can't afford *not* to read this book.

$18.95, 512 pp., 77 illus., ISBN 0-941188-05-1

Film Directing
SHOT BY SHOT
by Steven D. Katz

The most sought after book in Hollywood by top directors is filled with visual techniques for filmmakers and screenwriters to expand their stylistic knowledge. Includes storyboards from Spielberg, Welles and Hitchcock.

$24.95, 376 pp., 7 x 10
750 illustrations and photos ISBN 0-941188-10-8

INDEPENDENT FILM & VIDEOMAKERS GUIDE

by Michael Wiese

A classic best-seller and an independent producer's best friend. Advice on limited partnerships, writing a prospectus, market research, negotiating, film markets, pay TV and home video buyers.

$18.95, 392 pp., 45 illustrations, ISBN 0-941188-03-5

ORDER FORM

To order these products please call 1-800-379-8808 or fax (818) 986-3408 or mail this order form to:

MICHAEL WIESE PRODUCTIONS
11288 Ventura Blvd., Suite 821
Studio City, CA 91604
1-800-379-8808

BOOKS:

_____
_____
_____
_____

Subtotal $_____
Shipping $_____
8.25% Sales Tax (Ca Only) $_____

TOTAL ENCLOSED_____

Please make check or money order payable to
Michael Wiese Productions

(Check one) ___ Master Card ___ Visa ___ Amex

Company PO#_____

Credit Card Number_____
Expiration Date_____
Cardholder's Name_____
Cardholder's Signature_____

SHIP TO:

Name_____
Address_____
City_____ State_____ Zip_____
Country_____ Telephone_____

CALL 1-800-379-8808 for a Free Book & Software Catalog

VISIT OUR HOME PAGE http://www.earthlink.net/~mwp

_Please allow 2-3 weeks for delivery.
All prices subject to change without notice._

CREDIT CARD ORDERS

**CALL
1-800-379-8808**

OR **FAX**
818 986-3408

OR E-MAIL
WIESE@EARTHLINK.NET

SHIPPING

1ST CLASS MAIL
One Book - $5.00
Two Books - $7.00
For each additional book, add $1.00.

AIRBORNE EXPRESS
2nd Day Delivery
Add an additional $11.00 per order.

OVERSEAS (PREPAID)
Surface - $7.00 ea. book
Airmail - $15.00 ea. book